"This book is a very practical, comprehensive, and concise road map on how to approach growth in a strategic manner that aligns with a companies culture, core competencies, and external market potential opportunities. It presents the picture based on emerging trends and assesses opportunities based on risk tolerance and investment needed to advance those opportunities. The book is a must read for anyone seriously interested in growing as it entails a paradigm shift from inward thinking to customer and market focused thinking."

—Dennis Reimer, CEO,
Midwest Specialty Products

"Due to COVID-19, artificial intelligence, genetic sequencing, and blockchain, the world is changing faster than ever before, and the rate of change will never be this slow again! Perkins and Mazumdar provide you with the foresight to amplify weak signals that reveal opportunities along with threats to your business, while creating a roadmap to help you navigate from where you are today to where you need to be in the future. Packed with powerful insights and technological foresight, *The Innovation Engine for Growth* will enable you to not only survive but thrive in today's hypercompetitive world."

—Pete Dulcamara, Technical Vice President and
Chief Scientist, Kimberly-Clark Corporation

"This book is an important read in the innovation space. It covers many topics not often covered elsewhere, such as emerging innovation trends, opportunities and technologies across various industries. Since technologies, markets, and the competitive landscape are constantly changing, the authors provide a framework that can be used repeatedly as new opportunities arise."

—Marc J Epstein, Formerly business school
professor at Rice, Harvard, and Stanford Business
Schools and co-author Making Innovation Work:
How to Manage it, Measure it, and Profit from it

"This book is very informative and a great read. It provides an excellent overview of emerging technology and innovation trends in various market categories that could help in the identification of new business opportunities and provides a framework and the necessary tools to help in evaluation of these opportunities. This book is highly recommended for professionals focused on technology scouting, innovation and strategic planning/marketing."

—Robert M. Conforti, Ph.D., Vice President,
New Business & Technology Development,
Neenah Performance Materials

"The authors bring vast expertise to the pages of *The Innovation Engine for Growth*. This book highlights meaningful new ideas, fundamental concepts, as well as practical advice and case studies for anyone pursuing innovation."

—*Carlos Linares*, *EVP of Global R&D,*
Church and Dwight Co., Inc.

The Innovation Engine for Growth

Written by experts on innovation and growth, this book provides the necessary tools to systematically develop and sustain profitable innovation pipelines.

In a hypercompetitive global market, businesses must innovate to survive; yet the failure rate for innovation is extremely high. Strategists and thought leaders, Cheryl Perkins and Dr. Sanjay Mazumdar, offer a sophisticated yet practical approach for implementing successful innovation. Leveraging thought-provoking questions and powerful templates, the book outlines how companies can leverage core strengths, build internal innovation capabilities, partner effectively, and identify the promising areas to pursue. In addition, the book highlights emerging innovations in several major industries, providing fodder to fuel creative thinking and exploration of possible applications across a variety of different industries.

Managers and leaders will welcome the innovation insights and examples, as well as the templates to build an organization's plan to diagnose patterns of innovation, identify opportunities, and apply emerging innovations in their own industries and businesses.

Sanjay Mazumdar is CEO and Founder of Lucintel and is a published author, strategist, and thought leader. He has helped companies develop innovation pipelines and offered advisory services (M&A, market entry, strategic growth consulting, due diligence) to hundreds of clients for over 20 years as a CEO of Lucintel, which is a premier management consulting firm with over 1,000 customers from 70 countries.

Cheryl Perkins is CEO and Founder of **Innovation**edge, LLC and a global strategy and growth Thought Leader that helps companies achieve transformational innovation. One of *Business Week*'s "Top 25 Champions of Innovation", Cheryl previously served as Chief Innovation Officer for Kimberly-Clark, has 11 patents and more pending patents, and co-authored *Conquering Innovation Fatigue*.

The Innovation Engine for Growth

An Actionable Roadmap to Thriving in a Hyper-Competitive World

Sanjay Mazumdar and
Cheryl Perkins

NEW YORK AND LONDON

First published 2022
by Routledge
605 Third Avenue, New York, NY 10158

and by Routledge
2 Park Square, Milton Park, Abingdon, Oxon, OX14 4RN

Routledge is an imprint of the Taylor & Francis Group, an informa business

© 2022 Sanjay Mazumdar and Cheryl Perkins

The right of Sanjay Mazumdar and Cheryl Perkins to
be identified as authors of this work has been asserted
by them in accordance with sections 77 and 78 of the
Copyright, Designs and Patents Act 1988.

All rights reserved. No part of this book may be reprinted
or reproduced or utilised in any form or by any electronic,
mechanical, or other means, now known or hereafter
invented, including photocopying and recording, or in any
information storage or retrieval system, without permission
in writing from the publishers.

Trademark notice: Product or corporate names may be
trademarks or registered trademarks, and are used only for
identification and explanation without intent to infringe.

Library of Congress Cataloging-in-Publication Data
Names: Mazumdar, Sanjay K., author. |
Perkins, Cheryl A., author.
Title: The innovation engine for growth : an actionable
roadmap to thriving in a hyper-competitive world / Sanjay
Mazumdar and Cheryl Perkins.
Description: New York, NY : Routledge, 2022. |
Includes bibliographical references and index.
Identifiers: LCCN 2021012313 (print) |
LCCN 2021012314 (ebook) | ISBN 9781032012537 (hardback) |
ISBN 9781032012568 (paperback) | ISBN 9781003177906 (ebook)
Subjects: LCSH: Technological innovations—Economic
aspects. | Diffusion of innovations. | Success in business.
Classification: LCC HD45 .M376 2022 (print) |
LCC HD45 (ebook) | DDC 658.4/063—dc23
LC record available at https://lccn.loc.gov/2021012313
LC ebook record available at https://lccn.loc.gov/2021012314

ISBN: 978-1-032-01253-7 (hbk)
ISBN: 978-1-032-01256-8 (pbk)
ISBN: 978-1-003-17790-6 (ebk)

DOI: 10.4324/9781003177906

Typeset in Sabon
by codeMantra

Contents

List of Figures	ix
List of Tables	xiii
List of Templates	xv
Acknowledgments	xvii
About the Authors	xxi

Introduction	**1**
Getting the Most Out of This Book	**2**

SECTION I
Defining Your Strategy – Innovation for
Sustainable Growth   **5**

1 Three Horizon Framework for Short- and
Long-Term Growth   7

2 Core Strengths and Innovation Capabilities
Advancement   16

3 Strategic Partnerships and Their Role in
Accelerating Innovation   25

4 Socioeconomic Megatrends Driving Future Innovation   33

viii Contents

SECTION II
Identifying Opportunities, Partners, and Resources – Emerging Innovations by Selected Industries   49

5 Aerospace   51

6 Automotive   60

7 Chemical   71

8 Building Construction   92

9 Electronics   104

10 Internet of Things (IoT)   118

11 Medical Devices   131

SECTION III
Executing Your Strategy – Integrating Core Capabilities with External Opportunities   145

12 Summary   147

Conclusion: Mapping Your Plan   159

Index   173

Figures

1.1	Extended Horizon Model	8
1.2	Horizon Technology and Market Application	11
1.3	Innovation Ambition Matrix	13
1.4	Resource Allocation across Horizons	14
2.1	Innovation Capability Building Blocks	17
2.2	Strategy and Vision	21
2.3	Typical Cycle of Opportunity Identification and Innovation	22
3.1	Discovery Continuum Process	26
3.2	Growth Platform Definition	28
4.1	Socioeconomic Megatrends Affecting Business and Technologies	34
4.2	Aging Population Trend and Forecast across the Globe	36
4.3	Population Trends and Forecasts for Major Regions	37
4.4	Population Trends in Top Ten Populous Countries	37
4.5	Gross Domestic Product (GDP) Trends and Forecasts for Major Regions	38
4.6	Gross Domestic Products (GDP) in 2019 for Top Ten Largest Economies	38
4.7	Gross Domestic Product (GDP) Growth Rates for Top Ten Largest Economies	38
4.8	Internet Users across Regions	39
4.9	Mobile Subscriptions per 100 People across the World	40
4.10	Energy Demand across the Globe	41
4.11	Trends and Forecasts in Energy Demand by Region	42
4.12	Global CO_2 Emissions Trend	43
4.13	Global CO_2 Emissions by Major Countries/Regions	43
5.1	Key Innovation Areas for the Aerospace Industry	52
5.2	Emerging Innovations in the Aerospace Industry. (a) Fuel and Noise Efficient Aero Engine; (b) 3D Printing of Turbine Wheel; (c) Hybrid Airship; (d) Self-Cleaning Lavatory	53

5.3	Level of Technology Maturity by Innovation Category in the Aerospace Industry	55
6.1	Key Areas of Innovation Opportunity for the Automotive Industry	62
6.2	Emerging Innovations in the Automotive Industry. (a) Autonomous Cars; (b) Electric Vehicles; (c) Car Airbags; (d) Advanced Driver Assistance Systems; (e) Connected Cars	63
6.3	Level of Technology Maturity by Innovation Category in the Global Automotive Industry	67
7.1	Key Innovation Areas for the Coatings Market	73
7.2	Innovations in Nano-coatings Market. (a) Nano-Coatings for Electronics Device; (b) Nano-Coatings for Medical Implants	75
7.3	Key Innovation Areas for the Polymers Market	76
7.4	UV Light Curing of Automotive Adhesive	77
7.5	Applications of Structural Adhesives in Various Industries. (a) Automotive; (b) Aerospace; (c) Marine; (d) Wind	78
7.6	Composites Innovations in Various Applications. (a) Carbon Composite Wheel; (b) Aircraft Winglet	79
7.7	Key Innovation Areas for the Agriculture Market	80
7.8	Innovations in Advanced Seed Treatment	81
7.9	Level of Technology Maturity by Innovation Category in the Chemical Industry	84
7.10	Level of Technology Maturity by Innovation Category in the Coatings Market	85
7.11	Level of Technology Maturity by Innovation Category in the Polymer Market	85
7.12	Level of Technology Maturity by Innovation Category in the Agrochemicals Market	86
8.1	Intelligent Buildings	93
8.2	Key Areas of Opportunities in Innovation for the Construction Industry	94
8.3	Innovations in Green Building	95
8.4	Different Types of Advanced Manufacturing Techniques in the Construction Industry. (a) 3D Printed Structure; (b) Robots in Construction	96
8.5	Innovations in Advanced Materials for the Construction Industry. (a) Graphene; (b) GFRP	96
8.6	Innovations Accompanying the Idea of Compact Designing. (a) Compact Room Design; (b) Wall-Hung Dual-Flush Toilet	97

8.7	Level of Technology Maturity by Innovation Category in the Construction Industry	100
9.1	Key Innovation Areas in the Electronics Industry	105
9.2	Innovations in OLED TV	106
9.3	Innovations in Personal Robot	107
9.4	Innovations in Sensors. (a) Lidar Sensor; (b) Radar Sensor; (c) Wireless Sensor	108
9.5	Different Types of Energy-Efficient Devices. (a) Smart Lighting; (b) Smart Meter	108
9.6	Internet Connectivity	109
9.7	Miniaturization of Electronic Devices	109
9.8	Innovation in Big Data Technology	110
9.9	Innovations in Cloud Computing Technologies	111
9.10	Level of Technology Maturity by Innovation Category in the Electronics Industry	114
10.1	Key Innovation Areas for the IoT Market	120
10.2	Innovation Areas in IoT for Connected Homes	121
10.3	Innovation Areas in IoT for Smart Cities	122
10.4	Innovation Areas in IoT for Connected Wearables	123
10.5	Innovation Areas in IoT for Connected Cars	124
10.6	Innovation Areas in Industrial IoT	125
10.7	Level of Technology Maturity by Innovation Category in the IoT Market	128
11.1	Key Innovation Opportunity Areas in Medical Devices	133
11.2	Innovation Areas in Connected Health Devices. (a) BPM Monitor; (b) Personal ECG	134
11.3	Innovations in Advanced Prosthetics	136
11.4	Miniaturization of Medical Devices	137
11.5	Level of Technology Maturity by Innovation Category in the Medical Device Industry	140
12.1	Capabilities Advancement Approach for Increasing Company's Competitiveness	148
12.2	Top Innovation Areas and Future Revenue Opportunities	149
C.1	Innovation Capability Building Blocks	165
C.2	Growth Platform Definition	168
C.3	**Innovation**edge Growth Opportunity Framework™ Matrix	171

Tables

5.1	Innovation Opportunities in the Aerospace Industry	55
5.2	Horizon Planning Implications for the Aerospace Industry	57
6.1	Innovation Opportunities in the Automotive Industry	65
6.2	Horizon Planning Implications for the Automotive Industry	68
7.1	Market Opportunities of Various Innovations in the Chemical Industry	82
7.2	Horizon Planning Implications for the Chemical Industry	88
8.1	Innovation Opportunities in the Construction Industry	98
8.2	Horizon Planning Implications for the Construction Industry	102
9.1	Innovation Opportunities in the Electronics Industry	113
9.2	Horizon Planning Implications for the Electronics Industry	115
10.1	Innovation Opportunities in the IoT Market	127
10.2	Horizon Planning Implications for the IoT Industry	129
11.1	Innovation Opportunities in the Medical Device Industry	138
11.2	Horizon Planning Implications for the IoT Industry	141
12.1	Horizon Model in Top 14 Innovation Areas	150
12.2	Areas of Innovation, Technologies, and Ecosystems in Smart Cities	151
12.3	Areas of Innovation, Technologies, and Ecosystems in Powertrain Advancement	151
12.4	Areas of Innovation, Technologies, and Ecosystems in Electric Cars	152
12.5	Areas of Innovation, Technologies, and Ecosystems in Sensing Technologies	153
12.6	Areas of Innovation, Technologies, and Ecosystems in Safety and Security	153
12.7	Areas of Innovation, Technologies, and Ecosystems in Green Chemicals	154
12.8	Areas of Innovation, Technologies, and Ecosystems in Connected Cars	154

12.9	Areas of Innovation, Technologies, and Ecosystems in Advanced Automotive Electronics	155
12.10	Areas of Innovation, Technologies, and Ecosystems in Autonomous Cars	155
12.11	Areas of Innovations, Technologies, and Ecosystems in Advanced Materials	156
12.12	Areas of Innovation, Technologies, and Ecosystems in Connected Homes	156
12.13	Areas of Innovation, Technologies, and Ecosystems in Advanced Robotics	157
12.14	Areas of Innovation, Technologies, and Ecosystems in Connected Health Devices	158
12.15	Areas of Innovation, Technologies, and Ecosystems in 3D Printing	158
C.1	Innovation Ambition	164
C.2	Innovation Ambition and Resource Allocation	168
C.3	Growth Opportunity Matrix	170

Templates

C.1	Innovation Ambition	161
C.2	Team Competency Grid	161
C.3	Partner Competency Grid	161
C.4	Opportunity Impact/Ease Matrix	162
C.5	Opportunity Horizons	162
C.6	Innovation Value and Investment	163
C.7	Comparative Value	163
C.8	Innovation Growth Opportunity Matrix	164

Acknowledgments

Writing a book cannot be done alone and requires many months of sincere and focused work. None of this would have been possible without the candid and thoughtful input from our client partners and the thorough investigation and analysis from our teams. We are grateful to everyone who helped along the way.

My thank you list is big but in summary, I would like to thank all my clients with whom I have discussed game-changer ideas and the growth challenges they face as leaders in their respective domains. Working with over 1,000 small to large international clients across multiple industries during the last 20 years, I have gained insight into markets, competitive landscapes, and unmet needs in their value chains. These insights helped shape the contents of this book.

Big thanks to everyone at Lucintel, who enable me to be the CEO of a company that I'm honored to be a part of; thank you for letting me serve. Special thanks to Eric Dahl, Rajesh Padhi, and Dennis Kovalsky and their team who assisted me in research and analysis. Thanks to Tikaram Sahu, Kailash Soni, Irshad Ali, Vikash Sharma, Manasa Gantayat, Richa Sharma, Piyush Gautam, Richa Mishra, Leeann Powell, and Anne Christiansen, who contributed greatly to the research, analysis, and editing of this book.

I cannot overemphasize the importance of family members in writing this book. I thank my wife, Gargi Mazumdar, and my two lovely daughters, Dhriti Mazumdar and Roma Mazumdar, for helping me in my journey.

Being a spiritual person, I know that I could not have finished this book without God's blessing.

~ Sanjay

I personally am grateful for the tremendous support and input of clients, partners, colleagues, friends, and family. The approaches and frameworks in this book are drawn from working closely with top leaders throughout their journeys, from setting strategy to building high-performing teams, choosing partners, overcoming barriers, and ultimately achieving innovation and growth goals. I have shared the how-to's and factors contributing to success in this book. While there are too many individuals to list, I want to thank each and every one of them for their contributions to my journey.

I also want to profoundly thank those that directly contributed to the writing, editing, and overall shaping of the book's contents. A huge thank you to Pat Clusman, Kari Derks, Julie Gerstle, and the entire **Innovation**edge, LLC team. I also want to acknowledge Jackie Cooper's contribution in helping to structure the material to make it actionable for readers.

Finally, I deeply appreciate my husband, Mark, and my two sons, Matthew and Michael, for their support throughout my career even when it has meant time away from them. I feel fortunate to have been able to pursue my personal "innovation ambition" knowing they were there for me. I dedicate this book to them.

Writing this book has been a collaborative innovation experience in its own right – I deeply appreciate everyone's contribution and the wealth of knowledge that was shared.

~ Cheryl

Acknowledgments xix

The following tools, processes and models are copyrighted and trade-marked, as applicable, of Lucintel, LLC:

- Strategic Growth Consulting and Market Entry Roadmap
- Opportunity Screening and Analysis
- Commercial Due Diligence
- Market Analytics Dashboard
- Lucintel Product Innovation Award
- Lucintel Technology Innovation Award

The following tools, processes and models are copyrighted and trade-marked, as applicable, of **Innovation**edge, LLC:

- Extended Horizon Model
- Horizon Technology and Market Application
- Innovation Capability Building Blocks
- Strategy and Vision for a Company
- Typical Cycle of Opportunity Identification and Innovation
- Discovery Continuum Process
- Capabilities Advancement Approach for Increasing Company's Competitiveness
- Growth Platform Definition
- **Innovation**edge Growth Opportunity Framework™ Matrix
- Horizon Planning Implications
- Horizon Model in Top 14 Innovation Areas
- Innovation Ambition
- Innovation Ambition and Resource Allocation
- Growth Opportunity Matrix
- Innovation Ambition
- Team Competency Grid
- Partner Competency Grid
- Opportunity Impact/Ease Matrix
- Opportunity Horizons
- Innovation Value and Investment
- Comparative Value

About the Authors

Cheryl Perkins, CEO and Founder, Innovationedge, LLC

Cheryl Perkins is a widely acknowledged innovation expert and creative catalyst in brand-building initiatives. She has worked with many of the world's most successful companies to define and execute strategies that deliver sustainable growth and competitive advantage.

In 2006 *Business Week* magazine chose Cheryl as one of the Top 25 Champions of Innovation in the world. She was also named as a top executive driving vision within the consumer goods industry by *Consumer Goods Technology* magazine.

With over 20 years of experience directing growth and innovation, Cheryl previously served as Senior Vice President and Chief Innovation Officer for Kimberly-Clark. She ran the company's innovation and enterprise growth organizations, including research and development, engineering, design, new business, global strategic alliances, environment, safety and regulatory affairs, and oversaw innovation processes, systems, and tools. She has 11 US patents and several more pending.

Cheryl's first book *Conquering Innovation Fatigue: Overcoming the Barriers to Personal and Corporate Success* (co-authored with Jeff Lindsay and Muknd Karanjikar) was top rated on Amazon. She may be reached at cperkins@innovationedge.com

Sanjay Mazumdar, Ph.D., CEO, Lucintel

Dr. Sanjay Mazumdar is the CEO and Founder of Lucintel. He is a published author, strategist, and thought leader. He has helped over 500 companies with their growth objectives by developing market entry strategies and competitive advantage for over 1,000 markets/applications during the last 20 years. His expertise is in strategic growth, due diligence, market entry, M&A, and breakthrough innovation.

He has deep experience in technology and materials development in the chemical, composites, automotive, aerospace, construction, and electronics industries and has worked with companies such as 3M, BASF, Carlyle, Dupont, GE, GM, Mitsubishi, Sumitomo, and more. He received two Record of Inventions in his previous position at General Motors.

He received his Ph.D. in Mechanical Engineering from Concordia University, Montreal, and has additional training in Strategic Management from MIT, Cambridge. He received his Master's degree from I.I.T. Kanpur, India. He authored the book *Composites Manufacturing: Materials, Product & Process Engineering* – Publisher CRC Press (Taylor and Francis Group). He can be reached at Sanjay.mazumdar@lucintel.com.

Introduction

There is no debate – companies must innovate and grow to survive. As we enter a new decade, this pressure has become even more intense. The speed of technological change coupled with major socioeconomic shifts is unprecedented; organizations cannot sit still. They must be on top of emerging opportunities and threats – and ready to act swiftly.

The Innovation Engine for Growth was written to provide executives with a game plan to not just survive but thrive in today's hyper-competitive world. This book brings together the expertise of co-authors Cheryl Perkins, CEO and founder of **Innovation**edge, LLC, and Dr. Sanjay Mazumdar, CEO of Lucintel, who have 50 years of combined industrial experience helping over 1,000 companies successfully define and execute growth strategies. Cheryl's (**Innovation**edge, LLC) strategic insight and Sanjay's (Lucintel) market/technology foresight offer a complete picture of opportunities, potential collaborations, emerging innovation trends & developments, and the organizational capabilities necessary to compete.

DOI: 10.4324/9781003177906-1

Getting the Most Out of This Book

The book provides insights on innovation building capabilities, strategies for partnerships, innovation opportunities in a variety of industries, and more. Each chapter builds to shape a holistic roadmap that defines your organization's competitive advantage, identifies and ranks the most promising areas for your company to pursue, and maps these across three horizons for short-, medium- and long-term revenue growth. The **Innovation**edge **Growth Opportunity Framework** (IGOF)[1] *(Framework created and owned by **Innovation**edge, LLC)* outlined in the final chapter connects corporate strategy with emerging innovation opportunities.

As you read **Section I** (Chapters 1–4), it is suggested that you think and make notes about the following:

1. Your innovation ambition – how far do you want to push the envelope?
2. How much is leadership willing to invest? According to McKinsey, strong companies with good liquidity should pursue their most promising business opportunities and use the crisis to strengthen their long-term competitive position. "Companies that invested through previous downturns emerged stronger and were able to generate higher returns than competitors once the crisis was over[2]. *(Joint research from FCLT Global and the McKinsey Global Institute)*.
3. How do you allocate resources across core, incremental, and breakthrough efforts? (With COVID, it is imperative to control costs short term, but still allocate funds for long-term growth. The timetable for return on investment (ROI) and growth may be delayed but not reduced.)
4. What core strengths define your company's competitive edge?
5. What new capabilities will your organization need to develop or acquire to remain competitive? There is increased pressure to acquire new capabilities rapidly to meet new COVID-related demands. COVID-19 presents the opportunity for companies to tap into a

DOI: 10.4324/9781003177906-2

new talent pool with flexibility – one positive outcome of hiring freezes and unemployment.

6. What external resources (partners, suppliers, acquisitions, etc.) will help you reach innovation goals sooner and more cost-effectively? Stronger companies may be able to build capacity more cheaply or purchase assets at reasonable prices from weaker companies. During this period, well-capitalized companies can aggressively pursue M&A at attractive valuations (*McKinsey Global Institute*). In addition, a study conducted by *MIT Technology Review*[3] shows that businesses are building new capabilities and ecosystem partners (that is, extending what the company can do) and automating as much as possible – for reasons ranging from implementing physical distancing to providing more services online to coping with a smaller workforce. More than 55% of respondents are focusing on partnerships.

7. How robust is your current pipeline? How many new products/services/platforms will you be introducing over the next few years? Companies may want to bring ideas to market faster or acquire intellectual property from unexpected sources.

8. What are your current and future customers' needs and wants? This is difficult to predict, but COVID-19 has pushed many innovative ideas to the forefront for immediate action.

9. Which megatrends are most likely to affect your company's direction? In particular, the COVID outbreak has created a "touchless" megatrend which includes any economic activity performed without close interaction or being physically present in the place of the transaction. This will spur growth of industry 4.0, smart homes, robots, Internet of Things (IoT), and Artificial Intelligence (AI). Remote healthcare, public safety, sanitization, and many more areas are booming. Companies may find other untapped needs and opportunities as a result of this megatrend.

10. What is your organization's risk tolerance? Is experimentation encouraged?

As you read **Section II** (Chapters 5–11), the questions to bear in mind are:

1. Which emerging technologies in your industry (as well as adjacent industries) might enhance your current and future product lines?

2. Would their technology readiness and maturity work within your timeframe?

3. Which potential partners, resources, and ecosystems stand out as potentially strong fits for you? (Create a short list.)

4 Getting the Most Out of This Book

4. Who are your main competitors? Is there a need not being met by any of them?
5. Which opportunities align with your strengths?

Chapter 12 summarizes key findings about emerging trends and developments, and the **Conclusion** provides **Innovation**edge Growth Opportunity Framework (IGOF)[1] templates to build your organization's plan.

References

1. **Innovation**edge, LLC., **Innovation**edge Growth Opportunity Framework™
2. McKinsey, Navigating-COVID-19-Advice-from-long-term-investors.pdf
3. MIT Technology Review Insights, Amid-the-pandemic-shifting-business priorities_083120.pdf

Section I

Defining Your Strategy – Innovation for Sustainable Growth

To survive, organizations must stay on top of constantly changing markets, technologies, and socioeconomic factors. To be profitable, products and services must be continually enhanced while costs must be controlled.

Growth, however, requires more – a forward-looking strategy and the infrastructure to execute, a focus on the top line as well as the bottom line, and a steady stream of products and services that are new to the company and perhaps to the world. In short, innovation is necessary to thrive in the *future*.

This section explores ways to manage innovation as a whole and to achieve an optimum balance between short-term profit and long-term growth while strengthening your company's competitive position. Specifically, we outline four key factors to consider as you shape your organization's strategy:

1. **Plan for Long- and Short-Term Growth**. The Three Horizon framework ensures balanced resources across core, adjacent, and breakthrough business activities. Your company's vision combined with current and future customer needs will drive product portfolio decisions.
2. **Leverage Core Strengths and Capabilities**. Competitive advantage comes from leveraging and continually building your unique strengths and assets. **Innovation**edge has identified innovation capability building blocks that advance from product/service to digital innovation.
3. **Manage External Collaborations, Alliances, and Acquisitions**. Choosing the right external partners, suppliers, and ecosystems is critical to success. Alignment of goals, competencies, culture, and processes can make or break a collaborative effort.

DOI: 10.4324/9781003177906-3

6 Defining Your Strategy

4. **Tap into Megatrends.** Seeing where the future is headed in combination with your own customers' changing wants and needs helps you find expansion opportunities and white space. Moving quickly on emerging opportunities that fit your company's strengths enables early mover advantage.

Chapter 1

Three Horizon Framework for Short- and Long-Term Growth

Innovation is the cornerstone of competitive advantage and growth. The word "innovation" can mean many things, however. From a practical business perspective, our short definition is ***the creation and introduction of something new that generates economic value***. Economic value may come from products, services, systems, customer experiences, business models, ecosystems, channels, and more. The greater the benefits, the greater the value. Uniqueness and differentiation matter.

The challenge lies in identifying the specific innovations that will generate growth for an organization and build the capabilities necessary to deliver them. Further, the degree of innovation sought – extension, new to the company, or new to the world (disruptive) – adds complexity.

Not all innovation need be breakthrough or disruptive, but too much focus on near-term product and service improvements can stifle business growth in the long run. A healthy innovation continuum will address needs across multiple development horizons and align investment with risk/reward potential.

Typically, there are three degrees of innovation common to most industries.

- **Incremental** – improvements such as line extensions or feature updates
- **Sustaining** – higher-value creations yielding more competitive advantage
- **Breakthrough** – launching an entirely novel product or service

The Three Horizons model, introduced in the *Alchemy of Growth*[1], is used by many companies to define current, emerging, and future business opportunities. This model has many variations; at **Innovation**edge, LLC we have taken an extended view of the development horizons[2]. Our model addresses business development in three stages along a **product, technology, capabilities, services**, and **market development** continuum.

DOI: 10.4324/9781003177906-4

8 Defining Your Strategy

- **Horizon 1** activities generally address bottom line growth needs. Growth comes from maximizing the current profit picture.
- **Horizon 2** and **Horizon 3** activities both address top line growth. This growth comes from expanding the customer base and/or broadening product and service offerings. It includes expansion into new-to-the-company business areas (including new regions and geographies) and/or the creation of new-to-the-world products and services.

Planning along these horizons, in combination with building the right capabilities (discussed in Chapter 2), will help ensure the strategic and financial success of bringing new opportunities to market.

Implementing the Horizon Model

To begin with, it is helpful to describe each horizon more fully (see Figure 1.1). Each horizon definition relies on the same series of criteria. The criteria include product and service parentage, brand equity, technology, manufacturing requirements, timing, and capital investment. (Note that timing and capital investment criteria will be strongly affected by COVID-19 in the near term.)

Horizon 1

Horizon 1 addresses near-term, current market changes. Development in this horizon is the responsibility of the individual division or business unit. This horizon sustains your competitive edge and includes material

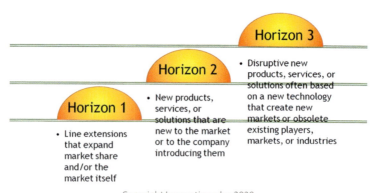

Figure 1.1 Extended Horizon Model.
Source: **Innovation**edge, LLC.

upgrades, product feature improvements, and upgrades. It also includes like-product line extensions.

The basis of **Horizon 1** products and businesses is current and/or improved technology that is easy to leverage. These products/businesses typically use current assets or slightly modified current assets.

Capital investment expenditures, if necessary, are readily justified. **Horizon 1** examples might include:

- Materials upgrade
- Technology upgrade
- Package upgrade
- Product feature improvement
- Product line extensions

From a market perspective, the consumer sees either no change (e.g. cost savings) or minor changes (e.g. line extension). Typically, these are tactical solutions to keep pace with competitors, to fill a gap, or to plug a sales shortfall.

Horizon 2

Horizon 2 addresses the crossover space between current and future development. Projects pass back and forth between the division or business unit and the new product development or venture unit as appropriate. There are links to the development needs adjacent to your current markets. It is the responsibility of the division or business unit to address the advancement of the business unit's competitive position. This includes repositioned base products, advanced materials and ingredients, and product design upgrades. This also includes near-term brand extensions.

Horizon 2 products and/or division or businesses rely on technology developed anywhere within the company. They may be based on outside technology but must be easily acquired (licensed or purchased) and integrated with current technology platforms. Most will use next or new generation assets. These assets must also be internal to the company or readily available for purchase. Manufacturing options include using outside vendors for production. Again, all capital investment requirements would be readily justifiable.

Horizon 2 examples might include:

- Repositioned base product/near-term brand extension
- Advanced material, technology, ingredient, product or package design upgrade
- New products (new to company, but not necessarily new to the world)

This horizon also begins to address the development areas outside your current markets. It is the responsibility of the new product development or venture team to stretch and expand the company's offerings by introducing new-to-the-company products, businesses, and services.

Horizon 2 also includes category improvements and/or novel offerings that require longer-term technology development. Shorter-term, advanced technologies that are new to the company may be integrated as well. In either case, the products in this horizon will not be easily or immediately integrated with *current* technology. New assets will need to be built, purchased, or leased.

From a market perspective, activities in **Horizon 2** meet an existing need in a new way or satisfy a previously unmet need. These activities represent a definable edge over the competition and may require the establishment of a new brand or allow a major extension of an existing product family within a brand. Typically, **Horizon 2** activities yield products which are new to a category or a market and include expansion to new regions and geographies.

Horizon 3

Horizon 3 developments are the responsibility of the new product development or venture team. These developments advance the company's competitive position by filling out the product offerings in entirely new spaces.

This horizon often includes category enhancements, new-to-the-world products, businesses, and services with new-to-the-world technologies. **Horizon 3** products will likely be a result of research investment through partnerships, joint venture developments, or venture capital spending. They will require new assets and technologies that are not part of your current portfolio.

Horizon 3 addresses products, services, or businesses which change the marketplace. They satisfy a previously unmet or unknown need and constitute a completely new market category/segment (e.g. latest mobile phones supplanting cameras). **Horizon 3** innovations can lead to early dominance in the new segment. At the same time, they can pose risks to the current business. Leaders need to assess the risk of cannibalizing their own business versus allowing a competitor to advance innovation in the targeted space.

Spanning the Horizons

Successful growth requires concurrent management across all three horizons. Companies typically use a platform model to illustrate the platforms being explored to deliver top line growth. To span the horizons,

	Technology	Market
Horizon 1	Exploitation of technology that is already widely understood and available. Only minor modifications required for delivery. Typical lead time <1 year. Easy to copy.	Consumer either sees no change (e.g. cost saving) or minor changes (e.g. line extension). Typically these are tactical activities to keep pace with competitors, to fill a gap in a range or to plug a sales shortfall.
Horizon 2	Marked improvements to existing technology, allowing significant product or process enhancement. May be adoption of technology from another industry or recombination of known technologies to yield new capabilities. May yield new patents. Typical lead time 2-4 years. Relatively difficult/expensive to copy.	Meets an existing need in a new way or satisfies a previously unmet need. Represents a definable edge over the competition and may require establishment of a new brand or allow a major extension of an existing product family within a brand. Typically yields products which are new to a category or a market.
Horizon 3	New to the world. Totally new technology, which gives a sustainable competitive advantage - likely to involve work with external agencies to develop new materials/equipment. Typical lead time 5-10 years. Deft patenting will make these developments difficult or impossible to copy.	Products which change the marketplace. Satisfies a previously unmet and unknown need and constitutes a completely new market category/segment (may satisfy needs previously met by other market segments e.g. latest mobile phones supplanting cameras). Can lead to early dominance in the new segment.

Copyright Innovationedge 2020

Figure 1.2 Horizon Technology and Market Application.
Source: **Innovation**edge, LLC.

each platform has one division or business unit sponsor and a business unit-based development liaison working with the new product development or venture team. This structure enables the team to maintain a strong linkage to the division or business unit. Many organizations apply this Horizon Model for growth to technology and market applications as illustrated in Figure 1.2.

Horizon 3 opportunities offer the greatest potential return on investment but carry the greatest risk. Exploration of breakthrough opportunities can be enhanced with the following approach:

- Anticipate and exploit early information through innovation processes such as laddering up, translating facts, trends, and observations into *big* insights, and creating growth platforms with mid- to long-term solutions. Focus on innovations that answer an identified need – not just technology.
- Experiment frequently, but do not overload teams with too many projects at once. Don't dilute efforts.
- Integrate new and traditional technologies, tools, and methods – this will create new capabilities while leveraging existing ones.
- Organize for rapid experimentation; fail "early and often," start small.
- Manage projects as experiments – test, adapt, re-test.

12 Defining Your Strategy

Each leadership team has its own level of risk tolerance. Leaders must communicate how far they are willing to go with novel solutions, and they must provide the support necessary to execute. Clarity, transparency, and consistent messaging are pivotal. Specific innovations processes, such as design thinking, are well documented in other works and not a focus of this book. **Innovation**edge, LLC has a comprehensive toolbox containing processes and templates to enable leaders to deliver capabilities from ideation, through the front end to the commercial pipeline.

Resource Allocation

Once the horizon structure is set, financial resources must be allocated. Important considerations include ambition level, pipeline/portfolio management, and short- vs. long-term emphasis.

1. Extent of Innovation/Ambition and Risk

    The degree of innovation ambition and risk will differ by industry, company size, and other factors. The **Innovation Ambition Matrix**[3], developed by Bansi Nagji and Geoff Tuff, is one of the most widely used tools to align investment across three levels of ambition. It is important to balance carefully among them to achieve total innovation management. The **Innovation Ambition Matrix** offers a framework for deciding "where to play" and "how to win" (Figure 1.3).

2. Pipeline Management

    Innovation and growth depend on continuous feeding of the pipeline along with ongoing mechanisms to ensure projects are sufficiently resourced. Again, the question of risk and reward comes into play across all three horizons. While H1 activities are usually managed with a stage gate process and projected return on investment (ROI) measures, H3 activities have inherent unknowns, which make investments purely speculative. Moreover, while pipeline management for core or near-adjacent innovation involves identifying a small set of winners from a large pool of ideas, transformational innovation works in the opposite direction, taking a few possibly game-changing ideas to make them viable. Before allocating resources, companies need to think about the full spectrum – number and time span of projects, degree of existing or to-be-acquired assets, risk tolerance, ROI, growth, and game-changing potential.

3. The 70-20-10 Rule and Alternatives

    There's no single ideal resource allocation model. That said, a commonly used rule of thumb is the **70-20-10 rule** where **70%** of resources go to **H1, 20%** to **H2,** and **10%** to **H3.** Popularized by Google years ago, the *70-20-10 allocation is also attractive to capital markets* because of what it implies about the balance between short-term predictable growth and longer-term bets.

Three Horizon Framework 13

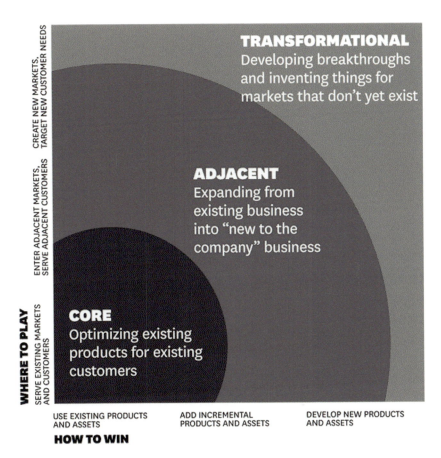

Figure 1.3 Innovation Ambition Matrix.
Source: Bansi Nagji and Geoff Tuff.

Not all companies use the **70-20-10** rule, however. Nagji and Tuff[3] share how different ambitions lead to different allocations (Figure 1.4):

> On average, high-performing firms direct 70% of their innovation resources to enhancements of core offerings, 20% to adjacent opportunities, and 10% to transformational initiatives. But individual firms may deviate from that ratio for sound strategic reasons. Here are three allocations we have seen that made sense for firms in various circumstances.
>
> One important factor is industry. The **industrial manufacturers**... have a strong portfolio of core innovations complemented by a few breakouts, and they come closest to the 70-20-10 breakdown.

14 Defining Your Strategy

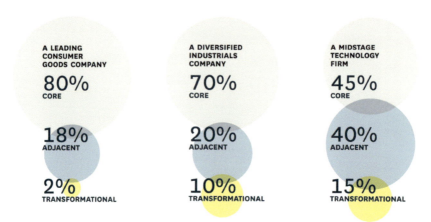

Figure 1.4 Resource Allocation across Horizons.
Source: Bansi Nagji and Geoff Tuff.

Technology companies spend less time and money on improving core products, because their market is eager for the next hot release. **Consumer packaged goods** manufacturers have little activity at the transformational level, because their main focus is incremental innovation.

Additional factors include a company's **competitive position** (lagging firms may strive for disruption) or **stage of development** (early-stage companies may want to make a splash; mature established firms will be sure to protect the core).

It is important to note that allocations and horizons are not permanently fixed. **Innovation**edge estimates allocations of **one year for H1, two to four years for H2, and five to ten years for H3**. COVID-19 has had a major impact on these timetables, however, as many companies have had to pivot virtually overnight to meet the changing environment. Some (such as providers of cleaning supplies) have increased core and incremental (H1) efforts, while others have had to bump up the timeline of new-to-the-business (H2) and breakthrough (H3) ideas.

The key is fluidity with some degree of stability; breakthrough initiatives generally require a much longer gestation period than core activities. Decisions and allocations in the COVID era also depend on a company's resources – liquidity, supply chain strength, and capabilities. There are no easy answers, but long-range sustainable innovation is still critical for growth.

Summary

Balancing short- and long-term is both an art and a science; mastering this balance is essential for sustainable growth. The Horizon model provides structure to maintain the "bread and butter" while building the future. It is based on three degrees of innovation common to most industries:

- **Horizon 1: Incremental** – including items such as line extensions or feature updates
- **Horizon 2: Sustaining** – higher-value creations giving more competitive advantage
- **Horizon 3: Breakthrough** – launching an entirely novel product or service

Resources should be allocated across all three horizons. These allocations will depend on how aggressive your growth goal is; for **moderate growth the 70-20-10 rule** is appropriate and for **accelerated growth the 40-40-20 ratio** would be more in order. As your portfolios evolve, adjustments are natural. The main caveat is to be sure changes have sound reasoning behind them, are transparently communicated, and not seemingly at whim or "out of the blue."

Build Your Roadmap[4]

1. Assess your current pipeline; number of projects in H1, H2, and H3.
2. What is your organization's innovation ambition? Where are you on the continuum of building the core to creating entirely new business?
3. How has COVID-19 affected your market? What breakthrough initiatives should you accelerate?
4. Are your resources allocated accordingly?
5. Which horizon(s) need additional resources to ensure growth?

References

1. Mehrdad Baghai, Steve Coley, and David White, "The alchemy of growth: Practical insights for building the enduring enterprise," Apr. 1999.
2. **Innovation**edge, LLC., Horizons Growth Model ©
3. Bansi Nagji and Geoff Tuff, "Managing your innovation portfolio," *Harvard Business Review*, May 2012.
4. **Innovation**edge, LLC., Build Your Roadmap ©

Chapter 2

Core Strengths and Innovation Capabilities Advancement

Companies with the capabilities to meet rapidly changing market needs are the ones best able to seize new opportunities.

In today's ultra-competitive and increasingly digital economy, these capabilities have become more complex. Advances in information technology and connectivity have heightened end-user expectations. Consumers want and expect products/services to "understand" them personally. They want 24/7 accessibility online, but they also want to see, touch, and feel products. They expect frictionless commerce and seamless delivery. Nothing less will do.

COVID-19 has put even more pressure on companies to build capabilities quickly. The need to transform products, services, and business models for an e-commerce-driven, safe, hygienic, and low-touch world requires strong **Digital Innovation** capabilities. Partnerships and acquisitions (see Chapter 3) are critical. It may be possible for financially stronger companies to make acquisitions at favorable rates due to COVID. A wider pool of talent may also be available as a result of layoffs and hiring freezes; nonetheless, it is important to choose wisely and adapt to remote collaboration models.

Innovation Capability Building Blocks

To compete in this environment, companies must be highly capable on several levels:

1. **Product/Service Innovation** to create offerings that ensure customer happiness
2. **Collaborative Innovation** for integration of new technologies and services
3. **Digital Innovation** to provide easy access, intelligence, personalization, and multi-channel delivery

While these capabilities overlap, they also build on each other and progress from product/service to digital innovation as follows (Figure 2.1).

DOI: 10.4324/9781003177906-5

Core Strengths and Innovation Capabilities 17

Figure 2.1 Innovation Capability Building Blocks.
Source: **Innovation**edge, LLC.

Product/Service Innovation Capabilities

Product/service innovation refers to the ability to define, develop, and deliver profitable new offerings, ranging from incremental to breakthrough. These capabilities include a wide range of capabilities such as people, teamwork, processes and tools, service, and portfolio management as described below.

People Capability/Skills: People skills such as creativity, drive, insight, pattern recognition, and market awareness are fundamental to innovation. Skill sets and personality traits of innovative people include:

- Sensitivity
- Asymmetrical thinking
- Sustained curiosity
- Dedication
- Fluency of thinking
- Flexibility
- Tolerance for ambiguity

Some of these skills can be taught but others are inborn. Hiring and retaining top talent is key, but it is also a challenge; career path, compensation, benefits, and work environment matter. The company's mission, values, and higher purpose matter too, especially to millennials. Cross-generational management is another challenge. Hands-on mentorships pairing older and younger team members can be an effective

18 Defining Your Strategy

way to transfer knowledge while simultaneously recognizing and acknowledging each generation's contribution.

<u>Teamwork:</u> Assign the right people to the right jobs and blend diverse and complementary talents. The mix of individuals should be chosen to ensure the right fit within the Three Horizon framework. In general, the characteristics to look for are as follows:

- **Horizon 1:** Ideally, those assigned to core and incremental activities will have strong operational and analytical skills. They will most frequently follow a gated process with an emphasis on time to market and cost efficiencies.
- **Horizon 2:** Teams are moving beyond what they currently know; they must be open to external opportunities with a solid understanding of business building as well as product and service development. Data interpretation skills and decision-making aptitude are necessary.
- **Horizon 3:** The people most suited for H3 are quite different from those for the other two horizons. They must be highly curious, creative, and positive, not afraid to push boundaries or take risks. They need to be strong enough to deal with failure and skepticism from others in the company.

Flexibility and ability to self-manage remotely are key in the COVID era across all functions and levels.

<u>Processes and Tools:</u> Develop processes, tools, and methods to gather data and insights; test hypotheses, concepts, and more. The latest tools and methodologies use advanced technologies such as data analytics, algorithms, machine learning, artificial intelligence (AI), and behavioral science to assist in data interpretation. Tools that can process and manage vast amounts of data are essential. Integration and management of information is a key capability.

<u>Customer Insight:</u> Successful innovation *must* be customer-driven and increasingly personalized. Organizations need to gather and interpret data from multiple sources, both online and in person. They must listen empathetically without bias to determine pain points, unmet needs, changing motivators, and the right problems to solve. Processes such as market research and design thinking can help.

<u>Service:</u> The way companies serve customers is key to competitiveness. Customers shift between channels (phone, email, chat, in store, social media, etc.) and even use multiple channels simultaneously. Firms therefore need an omnichannel communication strategy. Centralized access to customer and product information is essential for staff. Processes and "rules" must be clearly laid out, and representatives should

be empowered to do what's necessary. To continuously learn and improve, there must also be systems for tracking and measuring the customer experience. As service components are increasingly embedded in products or platforms and comprise the total customer experience, enterprises must transform operations with automation, AI, customer relationship management (CRM), case management, and other enterprise data stores.

Portfolio Management: It is important to focus on high-potential projects versus overloading the pipeline and diluting efforts. Identifying the most promising opportunities and making timely go/kill decisions are fundamental capabilities.

Collaborative Innovation Capabilities

Collaborative innovation takes product/service innovation to the next level. Through partnerships, acquisitions, incubators, and co-innovation centers, companies can acquire new capabilities, test new ideas, and accelerate delivery.

Building toward digital experiences requires ecosystems and multiple alliances to coordinate the full spectrum of services and technologies. (e.g. Kroger with Microsoft's retail-as-a-service platform, Instacart for same-day delivery, Home Chef meal kits, Ocado for e-commerce, etc.)

Internal collaboration must advance as well – R&D and marketing need to speak a common language and set unified goals. As software intelligence is increasingly embedded in hardware, development must be synchronized. Agile development methods (sprints, scrum, etc.) should be part of the process.

Digital Innovation Capabilities

Digital transformation has raised the stakes for product/service innovation. Delivering personalized customer experiences requires deep customer insight. Companies must determine what customers need now and will need in the future. This requires alignment between technology and business functions, including real-time data sharing and timely decision-making.

Being digitally capable also requires a greater degree of risk tolerance and sharper focus. Companies must prioritize between operational efficiencies and customer-facing experiences. While both can be accomplished simultaneously, the strategic intent will enable faster decision-making and better results.

The most critical skills[1] to develop are digital, analytical, and communications oriented. Companies will increasingly seek to hire data scientists, digital engineers, and analytics experts who understand both business and technology. Roles will include:

- Analytics and value managers who use data to inform decisions about pricing and value creation
- Business growth partners to act as a bridge between finance and the business units
- Accountants who can take financial, tax, and reporting processes, convert them into algorithms, and make sure that the algorithms are correct
- Global process owners to manage the standardization and implementation of technological platforms and working with outside vendors
- Data scientists to develop and implement simulations and models used to make decisions
- Digital engineers to develop new AI-based solutions for business challenges

The main technologies enabling digital transformation are data science, AI and machine learning, and the cloud.[2]

Data science helps to understand and optimize the customer journey. AI and machine learning are necessary for personalization and enhancing the customer experience. With machine learning, large amounts of data can be translated into insight and action. Finally, the cloud enables digital transformation and scalability on the infrastructure side.

Transformation leaders (such as Chief Digital Officers) will be instrumental in managing cross-functional projects, overseeing cultural changes, and continuously building capabilities.

Innovation Pipeline and Portfolio Management

The cycle of opportunity identification and innovation begins and ends with the customer, guided by corporate strategy and vision, and aligned with core capabilities and strengths (Figure 2.2).

To begin with, companies must ask the right customer questions and ensure that projects address problems worth solving (Figure 2.3). Critical questions to ask at the start of the journey include:

- Who is my target customer?
- What are their unmet or underserved needs?
- Where is the opportunity?
- What are the new benefits that can be created for these customers through new solutions?
- What is the customer's purchasing reasons to choose our offering over others?

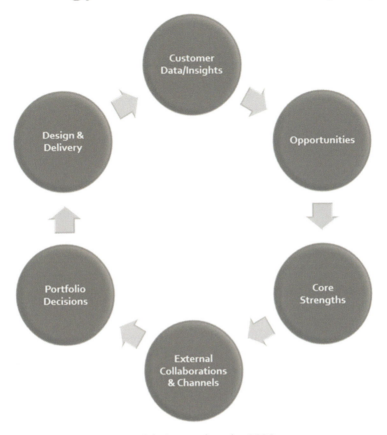

Figure 2.2 Strategy and Vision.
Source: **Innovation**edge, LLC.

Once these questions have been answered, the next step is to translate insights into development projects. Leaders must analyze the current business or service portfolio and decide which projects, businesses, and/or services to invest in. Effective portfolio management helps companies deliver on strategic goals through the prioritization of business opportunities, current projects, capabilities, and resources.

The most commonly used methods are matrices (such as the BCG Matrix, McKinsey, PPM) that weigh the contribution of different projects to the portfolio in terms of revenue, risk, investment required, and market

22 Defining Your Strategy

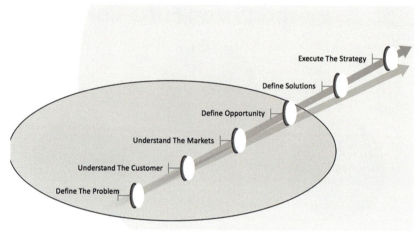

Figure 2.3 Typical Cycle of Opportunity Identification and Innovation. Source: **Innovation**edge, LLC.

leadership. The **Innovation**edge Growth Opportunity Framework[3] outlined in the final chapter of this book goes hand in hand with portfolio management but adds the multiple Horizon perspective.

Strategy and vision will ultimately guide opportunity selection – most opportunities will be sought, but others will present themselves. The seven main components of **Innovation**edge Opportunity Identification[4] are:

1. Strategic importance
   - Including the risk of doing nothing
2. Market attractiveness
   - Competitive advantage
3. Technology feasibility and synergies
4. Future growth potential (sustainability)
5. Capabilities of partner(s)
6. Financial risk versus reward
7. Intellectual Property (IP) assessment
   - All assets
   - Landscape
   - Freedom to operate

Capabilities of partners, technology feasibility, and IP assessment are part of Collaborative and Digital Innovation; choosing of the right opportunities depends on the other four factors and is the bridge between strategy and execution.

Capability Advancement

Overall organizational capability is achieved by continually building on existing competencies through leadership development, technical training/upskilling, knowledge sharing, mentorship programs, hiring and retaining top talent, partnering with and/or acquiring capable firms, updating tools and systems, funding/resourcing, and providing centralized access to data and insights. Project retrospectives ("post-mortems") as well as foresight sessions assure forward progress with the benefit of experience and lessons learned.

The role of leadership cannot be overemphasized.

At every level, function, and business unit there must be a culture of learning and experimentation, not fear. "Failures" must not only be acceptable, they should be expected. Openness, teamwork, and honest communication should be nurtured and rewarded. Metrics should favor experimentation and learning. The corporate vision and strategy must be articulated and well-understood. Decision-making should be informed but not cumbersome.

By having a clear short- and long-term innovation strategy (Three Horizons) combined with deep customer insight, people skills, partnerships, and delivery channels, organizations will be able to act quickly on opportunities and megatrends that align with their core strengths.

Summary

To recap, organizations must develop capabilities along a continuum:

1. **Product/Service Innovation** to create offerings and ensure customer happiness
2. **Collaborative Innovation** for integration of new technologies and services
3. **Digital Innovation** to provide easy access, intelligence, personalization, and multi-channel delivery

Capability development requires continuous updates to skills of employees, corporate knowledge, enabling technologies, and systems. The organizational ability to assess new opportunities and move decisively is the true "Engine of Growth."

Build Your Roadmap[5]

Candidly rank your organizations' competencies in each of these areas (1–5, 5 = superior). Refer to **Competency Grid templates**[6] in the final chapter of this book. Though these rankings are subjective, they will help you identify your key strengths and gaps to be filled:

_____ People Skills
_____ Teamwork
_____ Processes and Tools
_____ Customer Insight
_____ Service
_____ Portfolio Management
_____ External Collaboration
_____ Internal Collaboration
_____ Data Analytics
_____ Technology Proficiency (AI, machine learning, etc.)
_____ Agile Development

1. What are your top three strengths? Do any of these give you competitive advantage?
2. What are your biggest capability gaps? (Decide which you want to acquire externally and which you will build internally.)
3. Total your score – what is your overall capability score?

References

1. *Strategy + Business*, Jan. 7, 2019. HQ2.0: The Next-Generation Corporate Center, by Deniz Caglar, Vinay Couto, and Maureen Trantham.
2. *Information Age*, Jul. 16, 2018. Edge to Cloud: Digital Transformation and the Shifting Data Landscape, by Andrew Ross.
3. **Innovation**edge, LLC., **Innovation**edge Growth Opportunity Framework™
4. **Innovation**edge, LLC., Opportunity Identification Components ©
5. **Innovation**edge, LLC., Build Your Roadmap ©
6. **Innovation**edge, LLC., Competency Grid Templates ©

Chapter 3

Strategic Partnerships and Their Role in Accelerating Innovation

The pressure on businesses to expand and differentiate themselves creates numerous opportunities for innovation, not just in products and services but in entire business models and ecosystems. COVID-19 has exacerbated the pressure – and pivoting to meet current market demands and shifts has made partnerships almost mandatory.

Partnering is not easy, however. Despite rich opportunities for innovation that come from being open to the outside, companies have not been able to consistently deliver on results through these external relationships even before COVID.

Why is this so? How can a business turn outside innovation into successful new ventures? And what does it mean to be collaborative?

First, a company must be genuinely open to outside innovation and to sharing knowledge with others. A key characteristic of business ecosystems is that interactions involve more than a transaction of tangibles such as materials, products, and money. They involve the exchange of intangibles such as know-how, trust, loyalty, advice, and insight, which are vital to value creation as discussed in Chapter 1. Being open to innovation from the outside requires willingness to share such intangibles and to collaborate on multiple fronts.

Openness may even include collaboration with competitors. "Co-opetition" can, in fact, become a vital part of the business model and an excellent source of innovation. Companies should understand that it is possible to forge win/win paradigms with competitors as well as with consumers, regulators, and others and that these connections build competitive advantage.

The importance of open innovation is widely acknowledged. No one company has access to enough intelligence to create all the innovation it needs. Those on the cutting edge are increasingly reaching out to others – universities, vendors, allies and partners, customers, consumers, etc. – to find the ideas, skills, and assets that get them ahead.

DOI: 10.4324/9781003177906-6

Opportunity Discovery for Collaborative Innovation

Before engaging with outside collaborators, however, it is important to understand the overall playing field. Successfully building competencies, innovation pipelines, and future growth platforms requires a strategic approach to collaboration. **Innovation**edge, LLC's four-phase **Discovery Continuum Process**[1] (illustrated below) enables you to gain broad knowledge about the competitive landscape and opportunity areas while uncovering specific ideas and technologies. This knowledge enables you to not only identify prospective partners, but to create differentiated offerings (Figure 3.1).

The four phases are **Exploration, Scouting, Prospecting,** and **Mining**.

1. Exploration
    The first step in seeking collaborative business opportunities is to gather information. Explore places (geographic regions, universities, labs, conferences/expos, start-ups, etc.) and resources such as journals, RSS feeds, Google.
    Look for:
    - New landscapes
    - New opportunities, including areas of unmet and underserved customer needs

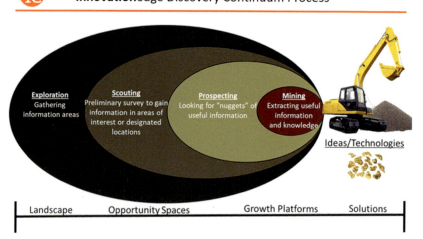

Figure 3.1 Discovery Continuum Process.
Source: **Innovation**edge, LLC.

- Competitive intelligence
- Market intelligence

2. Scouting

The next step is to systematically gather information for technology sourcing – either directed at a specific technology or undirected to uncover white spaces. This step relies on formal and informal information sources, including personal networks of the scouts. This phase goes beyond initial exploration to include Intellectual Property (IP) and developing a vision for what could be; think about consumer-centric targets and commercial applications.

3. Prospecting

After identifying key opportunity areas, prospecting is the physical search for actionable information, data, facts, resources, and technologies. This step is focused and deep. Once the field is narrowed, you can begin focusing on concepts to develop and stake your IP claims early.

4. Mining

Mining involves filtering the information gained and extracting tangible value. Processes involve prospecting for the right information, analyzing the potential, extracting the desired value and preparing it for business use.

The overall goal is to match external technologies and internal requirements to fuel ideas so they can eventually be converted into revenue-producing solutions. The **Growth Platform Definition**[2] below illustrates the process further.

Growth Platform Definition

Innovation in the COVID-19 Era

As a result of COVID-19, the **Innovation**edge, LLC's Opportunity Discovery Process[3] is accelerated (Figure 3.2). Crises force new ways of thinking, and innovation can soar if unknowns are embraced. Key points to bear in mind:

- **Ends, not means, drive the process** – the presence of a challenging vision compels innovation, even if the ways of reaching the goal are unclear.
- **Extensive search** – because the normal pathways may be blocked the search for solutions pushes out into new and unfamiliar territory. Don't limit yourself to past resources.
- **Reframing** – see the problem from a fresh perspective; new problems lead to new solutions.
- **Creatively combining** – improvise solutions from what is available, often in novel configurations.

28 Defining Your Strategy

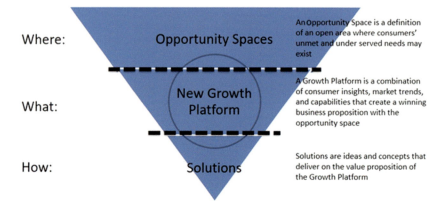

Figure 3.2 Growth Platform Definition.
Source: **Innovation**edge, LLC.

- **Experimental learning** – improvise and build on what emerges, using early prototyping and fast intelligent failure.
- **Small, imperfect steps matter** – tolerance of imperfection and incremental continuous improvement toward an optimal solution will encourage more creative risk-taking.

Open Innovation

With the knowledge gained, you can turn to those in your current value network to discuss expansion opportunities and capabilities. These strategic value networks may include a wide variety of partners, customers, experts, and outside thought leaders for each of the designated areas. You may wish to turn first to groups that you already trust, while reaching out to others identified through the discovery process. This approach has the virtue of offering a broad perspective, building ecosystems, and accelerating innovation with best-in-class partners.

Keep in mind that open innovation not only results in the creation of new product offerings, it can drive significant improvement in innovative practices by your vendors and suppliers. You can obtain information, guidance, and advice from the members of your external networks, and in return they learn more about your operations and might even be given a voice in certain decisions.

Similar approaches, often on a much smaller scale, can make sense for many businesses. Again, a holistic approach facilitates open innovation pursuits with an appropriate level of financial risk. With a sound holistic approach, all parties gain financially and strategically.

Choosing the Right Partnership Model

As executives in all sectors today strive to make their organizations leaner, it can be challenging to allocate the time, talent, and resources needed for continual and rapid innovation. However, external partnerships and alliances can drive innovation and growth while simultaneously reducing risk and costs with the right resource combinations and economies of scale.

Developments in the areas of information and communication technologies also create options for increasing capability and capacity – often without adding fixed costs. Consequently, many leaders today are exploring technology combinations through **strategic partnerships and alliances**. However, some situations lend themselves to **outsourcing** rather than partnering. There are different models that make sense for different circumstances, and each must be evaluated in terms of specific goals.

Partnerships and alliances can enable extended value chains, entrance into new markets, and expansion of existing distribution channels, as well as many other advantages. However, there can also be disadvantages – choosing wisely is critical.

A good first step is to **assess the internal competencies** (see Chapter 2) required to deliver on current or anticipated future objectives and goals. By examining your current ecosystem and defining current and future needs, you can identify gaps and see where potential partners might close those gaps.

Competency assessment is a three-part process:

1. **Competency Grids**[4]
    Competency grids include criteria ranging from behavioral and leadership competencies to specific technical competencies, often within a variety of disciplines. Comprehensive grids allow senior leaders to evaluate individual and organizational performance from multiple perspectives, including performance-related to specific programs, projects, or products. (Note: Competency Grid templates are provided in the Conclusion chapter.)
2. **Competency Grid Discussion**
    Once you have created a competency grid for your own organizations, the same template should be given to potential partners, and they should be asked to construct competency grids as well. Then each party should review, discuss, and share examples and references that can validate the specific competencies identified.

30 Defining Your Strategy

3. **Due Diligence**

To ensure that potential partners have the required competencies, you must then conduct due diligence to determine whether potential partners are a good fit. If partnerships demand cultural compatibility, you should determine the degree and nature of the differences to decide whether culture change needs to be driven in one or both organizations. On a final note, you can prevent or mitigate problems with "partners of partners" by performing the same due diligence on partners' networks that they've done for the partners themselves – including competency grids and validation from examples and references.

At the same time, it is important to clearly define business needs or business propositions and make sure partnerships are viewed from a well-rounded perspective, not just the technology or ideas to be acquired.

Pitfalls to Avoid

In addition to choosing the wrong partner(s) or focusing too narrowly on outcomes, pitfalls can occur when leaders in one or both companies err on how they structure the deal. Leaders need to make sure they have mutually agreed-upon objectives and that they structure partnership models or arrangements in ways that match the risk tolerance of both parties.

Finally, and perhaps most importantly, problems can occur if either party isn't able to manage the required culture change or lacks the ability to manage relationships. Sometimes organizations attempt to protect their IP by keeping partners at arm's length. This lack of engagement usually stalls relationships from developing and ultimately produces trust issues. Even in a best-case scenario, these behaviors can prevent deliverables from being realized or realized within desired timelines. The most effective way to protect IP is when both parties define what they need to own prior to engaging in the relationship. Leaders shouldn't have the expectation that any one partner will meet all needs; often market access is enough to ensure commercial success. During initial collaborations, however, both parties should define what IP is currently owned, what needs to be owned by each, and what will be jointly owned in the future.

Organizational Considerations

Specific types of partnerships and desired outcomes determine changes that might be needed in organizational structures, processes, and practices. Often leaders hire alliance managers with excellent decision-making abilities to manage complex relationships and to drive organizational change. These individuals play a critical role in ensuring that results are delivered within agreed-upon timelines and budgets, and that the relationship and desired behaviors remain intact over time.

They can often raise awareness about events, systems, and attitudes that shut down innovation. Skepticism, distrust, and a lack of sharing are silent killers of innovation. Silent, because in these situations, people often go through the motions – appearing to be on board and driving innovation – when, in fact, they have not bought in and might be undetectably disinterested or intimidated. In some cases, people might hold back or save their best ideas for other "safer" opportunities or for those aligned with political agendas. While innovation might remain the mantra in these circumstances, people might only welcome familiar kinds of innovation from insiders or trusted allies. The "not-invented-here" (NIH) syndrome is one of the most common barriers facing innovators, and it can occur at many levels.

Although NIH often manifests as an organizational or process issue, it is usually a matter of politics or unhealthy human pride, which fortunately can be remedied. Effective alliance managers and skilled leaders can overcome or offset NIH by demonstrating how partnerships will ease workloads and enrich the organization. Further, recognizing and rewarding individuals and teams for embracing external perspectives helps reduce fear and resistance.

Finally, after identifying competencies, conducting due diligence, and structuring partnership or co-development arrangements, leaders need to manage portfolios appropriately with balanced levels of risk. When culture change is required, they must deploy effective change management strategies that secure buy-in and sponsorship. Ultimately, the most important factors in sustaining mutually beneficial partnerships are: (1) communicating extensively and transparently, and (2) being clear about goals and being mutually trustable to deliver quality results on time and within budget.

Summary

The benefits of external collaboration are significant. Differentiated and meaningful innovation can be accelerated. Unique capabilities and competencies of partners can be combined so the sum is greater than its parts. Market reach and distribution can be expanded. New ideas can be tested more readily. Since risk and resources are shared, current resources can be re-deployed to pursue new opportunities.

Unfortunately, partnerships don't always meet expectations. To partner successfully:

- Invest time up front to identify and select partners that meet **defined criteria** for expertise, risk tolerance, presence in certain markets, and other key factors.

- Create **competency grids** that each partner fills and reciprocally discusses.
- Conduct thorough **due diligence**.
- Recognize the importance of **culture compatibility**. Pay attention to the nuances, be flexible, and show respect for the unique attributes each organization brings.
- Appoint an **alliance manager** to oversee complex relationships and drive necessary organizational changes.

Build Your Roadmap[5]

1. Review your ambition/risk profile (Chapter 1) to identify horizon needs that might be met through partnerships.
2. Review your capability assessment (Chapter 2). What non-core activities might be outsourced? What core capabilities might be built through acquisitions, mergers and/or alliances? Where do you need to accelerate capability building?
3. List potential areas of innovation and growth where external resources are needed.
4. Create a competency grid to assess your strengths and those of potential partners; assess synergistic strength as well as potential conflicts. (Templates provided in Conclusion chapter.)

References

1. **Innovation**edge, LLC., Discovery Continuum Process™
2. **Innovation**edge, LLC., Growth Platform Definition ©
3. **Innovation**edge, LLC., Opportunity Discovery Process™
4. **Innovation**edge, LLC., Competency Grids ©
5. **Innovation**edge, LLC., Build Your Roadmap ©

Chapter 4

Socioeconomic Megatrends Driving Future Innovation

In this chapter, we will study seven socioeconomic megatrends, which may likely have the biggest impact on innovation through 2050. These seven trends are (1) healthcare expansion, (2) changing demographics, (3) global power shifts, (4) ubiquitous connectivity, (5) increasing energy demands, (6) climate change, and (7) automation/digitalization. As a result of COVID-19, new megatrends have emerged within these major megatrends – particularly in healthcare and automation/digitalization. The "Touchless" or "Low Touch" economy has affected all industries, however. Safety, cleanliness, and minimal and/or distant human contact have become essential components in nearly every product or service.

In the next section, we will be highlighting the implications, followed by more details and statistics for each of the above seven megatrends, as given below. Some megatrends will present growth opportunities; others are mandatory for regulatory reasons (Figure 4.1).

Highlights

1. **Healthcare Megatrends**[1]: The aging population and rising healthcare spending will fuel expansion; technological advancement and innovation will continue at a rapid pace. In addition, new consumer-driven wellness trends (such as preventive medicine, nutritional awareness, supplementation, nutraceuticals, wearables, genetic testing kits, etc.), are driving innovation. *Advanced and intelligent medical technologies are creating new markets and causing rapid obsolescence of existing solutions. COVID-19 is accelerating the push for technology innovation in remote healthcare delivery, immunity, hospital care, diagnostics, personal protective equipment and more.*

2. **Population and Demographic Megatrends:** Demographics and the age structure of the world's population are changing dramatically. The decline in population growth rate due to fertility reduction and increased life expectancy has created a much higher proportion of

DOI: 10.4324/9781003177906-7

34 Defining Your Strategy

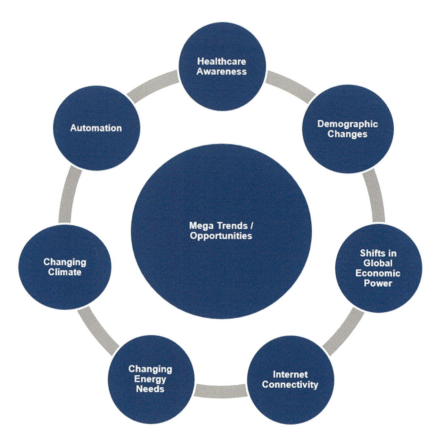

Figure 4.1 Socioeconomic Megatrends Affecting Business and Technologies. Source: Lucintel.

older persons in many countries. ***Different demographics and age dynamics are creating new needs and opportunities on both the local and the global level.***

3. **Shifts in Economic Power:** By 2050, it is forecast that the global economy will be led by China with India in second place. Emerging markets (E7 – China, India, Brazil, Mexico, Russia, Indonesia, and Turkey) are expected to grow twice as fast as advanced economies (G7 countries – Canada, France, Germany, Italy, Japan, the United Kingdom, and the United States). **The impact of these shifts should be factored into long-term growth planning, particularly in terms of needs and cost considerations for emerging markets.**
4. **Internet Connectivity and IoT[2] (Internet of Things) Megatrends:** The Internet has revolutionized communication and interaction

across industry. Connected homes, connected health, smart cities, connected cars, and industrial internet are just the beginning; *the IoT market for innovation will continue to soar.*

5. **Energy Megatrends**[3]: Energy demand is increasing dramatically as a result of the growing population and more urbanization. It is forecast that the world will need 50% more energy by 2050. *The innovation trend is moving away from fossil fuels to alternative energy sources such as renewable energy and battery technology.*

6. **Climate Change Megatrends:** It has become imperative for every country to help mitigate the global warming effects of unpredictable weather patterns and rising sea levels. CO_2 emissions control is crucial and most countries have regulations in place. *Predominant innovation trends are the development of fuel-efficient vehicles, energy-efficient homes, pollution-free chemical plants, and the utilization of green and sustainable chemicals/products.*

7. **Automation**[4,5]**: and Digitalization Megatrends:** From automotive to industrial and healthcare, *automation/digitalization is the biggest trend shaping the future. Digitalization* is the use of digital technologies to change a business model and provide new revenue and value-producing opportunities; it is the process of moving to a digital business. Digital technologies include artificial intelligence, machine learning, IoT, robotics, sensors, voice recognition, augmented reality, and more.

During the COVID-19 outbreak, we have seen significant trends in automation and digitalization, which is creating the need for a touchless economy. For example, during the quarantine period, we have seen a shift toward online meetings, online education, telemedicine, and online shopping from Amazon, Flipkart, etc., to reduce human contact. We are also seeing an increased demand for robots in hospitals, factories, and daily life. We are also expecting a shift toward flexible and smart manufacturing, which can help part fabricators to maintain a balance between their inventory and actual demand.

Details/Statistics

Healthcare

The global population is growing from 1 billion people over age 60 in 2019 to 2.1 billion by 2050. This surging population poses major challenges to the healthcare systems as medical[6] spending rises with the increase in individuals' age (Figure 4.2).

By the year 2030 more than 20% of the US population will be above 65 years. It is expected that China will have more than 390 million persons

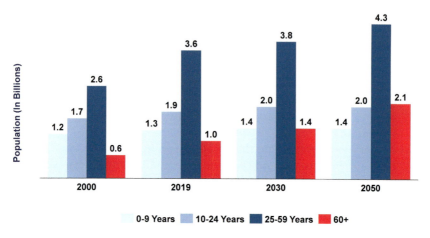

Figure 4.2 Aging Population Trend and Forecast across the Globe.
Source: Lucintel.

above 65 years by 2050. Overall, the aging population and rising healthcare spending will fuel expansion; technological advancement and innovation will continue at a rapid pace. At the same time, individuals of all ages are turning to consumer-oriented wellness offerings (such as yoga, meditation, preventive medicine, nutritional awareness, supplementation, nutraceuticals, wearables, genetic testing kits, etc.) not generally covered by insurance. The consumer-based wellness trend will drive innovation in delivery and services and create opportunities across industry.

Population and Demographic Megatrends

World population and demographics are changing dramatically, leading to new opportunities around the world. The decline in the population growth rate due to fertility reduction and increased life expectancy has created a much higher proportion of older persons in many countries, though some countries such as India have a relatively large population under 25 years.

Figure 4.3 shows population trends by region. Overall, the world population is forecast to reach 10.8 billion in 2050 from 7.7 billion in 2019. Asia had the highest population in 2019, followed by Africa. The ten most populous countries are China, India, the United States, Indonesia, Brazil, Pakistan, Nigeria, Bangladesh, Russia, and Japan (Figure 4.4).

Shifts in Economic Power

World economic centers are changing. By 2050, the global economy is forecast to be led by China, with India in second place. Also, emerging markets (E7 countries including China, India, Brazil, Mexico, Russia, Indonesia,

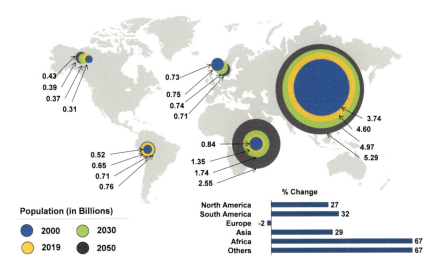

Figure 4.3 Population Trends and Forecasts for Major Regions.
Source: Lucintel.

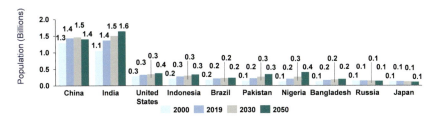

Figure 4.4 Population Trends in Top Ten Populous Countries.
Source: Lucintel.

and Turkey) are expected to grow twice as fast as advanced economies (G7 countries of Canada, France, Germany, Italy, Japan, the United Kingdom, and the United States). The impact of these shifts in economic power must be factored into long-term growth planning. The world's gross domestic product (GDP) is forecast to reach $257 trillion in 2050 from $94 trillion in 2019. Emerging markets will drive global financial growth and progressively increase their share of world GDP. Figure 4.8 depicts the trends and forecasts for GDP by major regions globally. Asia has the highest GDP in 2019, followed by North America (Figure 4.5).

Figures 4.6 and 4.7 show the ranking of the top ten economies and their respective growth rates.

In the long term, global economic power is expected to shift away from the advanced economies to emerging market countries, which continue to boost their share in the world GDP despite recent mixed

38 Defining Your Strategy

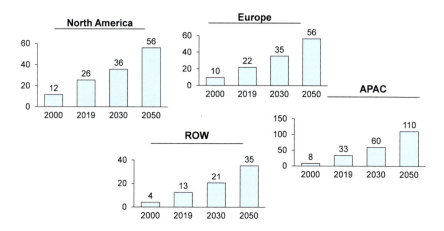

Gross Domestic Product (In US $Trillions)

Figure 4.5 Gross Domestic Product (GDP) Trends and Forecasts for Major Regions.
Source: Lucintel.

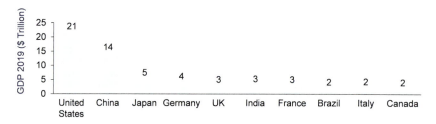

Figure 4.6 Gross Domestic Product (GDP) in 2019 for Top Ten Largest Economies.
Source: Lucintel.

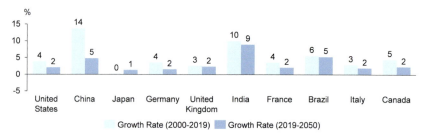

Figure 4.7 Gross Domestic Product (GDP) Growth Rates for Top Ten Largest Economies.
Source: Lucintel.

performance in some of these economies. Countries that currently have low productivity levels (India, China, Indonesia, Brazil, and those in Eastern Europe) are projected to grow faster as they catch up with developed economies. In terms of GDP growth, China and India are projected to grow rapidly before slowing down progressively in later decades as they mature.

Expansion into growing economies presents innovation opportunities in the development of low-cost products such as diapers, feminine sanitary products, medical equipment, vehicles, and other basics for emerging markets where the average salary is less than $10,000.

Internet Connectivity/IoT

The internet has had the biggest impact on society over the past decade, revolutionizing communication and interaction in every facet of daily life. In 2000, there were fewer than 0.3 billion internet users across the globe and slightly fewer people with connections. Today the number of users has reached approximately 4.2 billion. These numbers are forecast to climb to 5.6 billion by 2030.

Figure 4.8 shows the trends and forecasts of internet users by region. Internet users are growing at a faster pace in developing nations, whereas developed nations such as North America and Europe have reached the point of saturation. Asia and Latin America are expected to register slow growth, whereas Africa and Oceania will grow at a good pace over the forecast period.

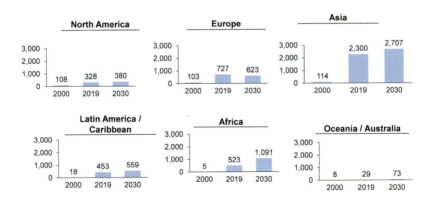

Internet Users (In Millions)

Figure 4.8 Internet Users across Regions.
Source: Lucintel.

40 Defining Your Strategy

Mobile phones have become integral to all forms of communication. As the number of mobile phone users continues to rise, the number of mobile phone subscriptions per 100 people is expected to hit 140 in 2030 and 160 in 2050, up from 113 in 2019 and 12 in 2000. Figure 4.11 shows mobile phone user growth around the world from 2000 to 2050.

There are now billions of mobile phone and internet users on the planet and different socioeconomic classes have different purposes; those in lower socioeconomic classes tend to focus on basic communication, education, and research, whereas those in higher socioeconomic brackets take advantage of online shopping, banking, and other conveniences (Figure 4.9).

The increase in internet and mobile usage has driven a proliferation of equipment and devices. There are now billions of physical devices around the world that are connected to the internet, collecting and sharing data. The availability of low-cost processors and wireless networks has enabled IoT products and services for almost any application. Connected homes, connected health, connected cars, smart cities, and the industrial internet are the primary growth markets. We have one whole chapter dedicated in Section II to discuss various innovation areas in IoT.

Energy

Significant changes in energy demand are occurring as a result of increased population and urbanization. The world will need 50% more energy by 2050 as compared to 2019 and the trend is away from fossil

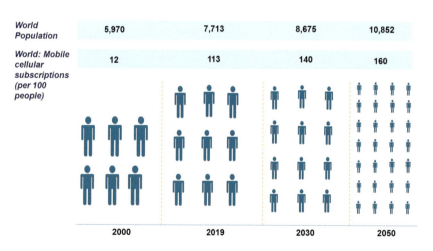

Figure 4.9 Mobile Subscriptions per 100 People across the World.
Source: Lucintel.

fuels toward alternative energy sources such as renewable energy and battery technology. Further, energy is becoming more decentralized, decarbonized, and digitized. Pressure from consumers, investors, and regulators are requiring companies worldwide to reduce their environmental footprints and develop sustainable energy solutions. This will lead to more renewable energy sources in the grid. In addition, IoT developments will bring interconnectivity to help companies and consumers make better decisions in response to real-time grid signals.

The world energy demand is forecast to reach ~23 Btoe in 2050 from 13.9 Btoe in 2018. The robust global economy, increasing population, and greater usage of advanced technologies are continuously pushing energy demand. To meet this demand, companies are using oil, natural gas, coal, renewables, nuclear energy, and other sources. In different regions across the world, it is expected that growing energy needs will be met mostly by renewables and natural gas, followed by other sources (Figure 4.10).

Developed nations such as North America and those in Europe have shown steady growth in energy demand in the past and are expected to maintain a similar pattern over the forecast period, whereas developing regions such as the Middle East, Africa, and Asia are expected to register double-digit growth rate, as shown in the Figure 4.11.

Finally, the energy mix is shifting, driven by technological improvements and environmental concerns. For example, 18% of the energy consumed globally for heating, power, and transportation was from renewable sources in 2017. Nearly 60% came from modern renewables (i.e. biomass, geothermal, solar[7], hydro, wind, and biofuels) and the remainder from traditional biomass (used in residential heating and cooking in developing countries). Regarding global electricity generation, renewables made up 26.2% in 2018. That's expected to rise to 45% by 2040. Most of the increase will likely come from solar, wind,

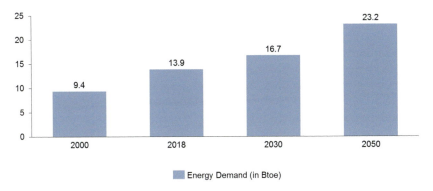

Figure 4.10 Energy Demand across the Globe.
Source: Lucintel.

42 Defining Your Strategy

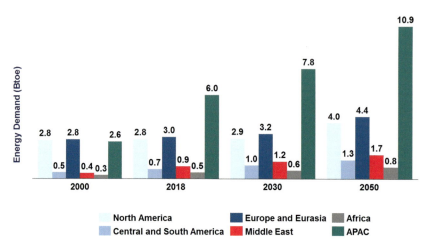

Figure 4.11 Trends and Forecasts in Energy Demand by Region.
Source: Lucintel.

and hydropower. The source of energy is key to sustainability and there is a push toward renewable energy, particularly solar and wind energy, which provide a source of energy/electricity without giving rise to any carbon dioxide emissions.

Climate Change

This megatrend is one that no company can ignore. The environmental, social, and economic implications of greenhouse gas emissions are enormous; most countries have emission-related regulations in place. This is driving innovation in fuel-efficient vehicles, energy-efficient homes, pollution-free chemical plants, and utilization of green and sustainable chemicals/products. The largest source of greenhouse gas emissions from human activities in the United States is from burning fossil fuels for electricity, heat, and transportation.

Greenhouse gases like carbon dioxide (CO_2), nitrous oxide (N_2O), and methane (CH_4) trap heat in the atmosphere. With higher-than-natural concentrations, they lead to unnatural warming. Activities such as burning of oil, coal, and gas and deforestation are the major causes of increased CO_2 concentrations in the atmosphere. China, the United States, the European Union, and India are the top countries emitting CO_2, as shown in Figure 4.12. These largest emitters have a larger role to play in determining the climate of the future. Population and size of the economy are the two major drivers of emissions. Figures 4.12 and 4.13 show the CO_2 emissions in the world and by regions from 2000 to 2019, indicating growth of more than 2% CAGR.

Socioeconomic Megatrends 43

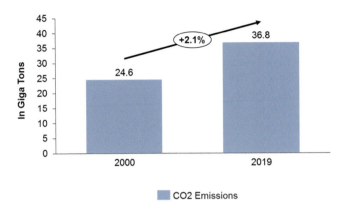

Figure 4.12 Global CO_2 Emissions Trend.
Source: Lucintel.

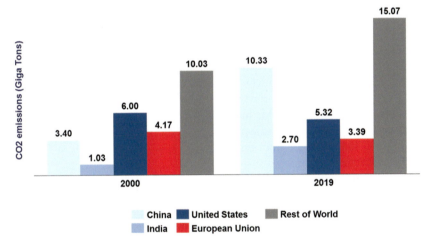

Figure 4.13 Global CO_2 Emissions by Major Countries/Regions.
Source: Lucintel.

The United States: The largest source of GHG emissions in the United States is from burning fossil fuels for electricity (mostly coal and natural gas) and transportation (cars, trucks, ships, trains, and planes). Multiple measures were taken to reduce emissions from fossil fuel combustion, including substitution from coal to natural gas consumption.

EU: In Europe, many countries have adopted national programs aimed at reducing emissions, such as:

- Increased use of renewable energy (wind, solar, biomass) and combined heat and power installations

44 Defining Your Strategy

- Improved energy efficiency in buildings, industry and household applicances
- Reduction of CO_2 emissions from new passenger cars

China: As one of the largest CO_2 emission countries and one of the most populated countries, China is putting more and more effort into combating climate change. Some of the major initiatives taken to reduce GHG emissions are limiting the use of coal by shutting down existing coal mines, cutting pollution from automobiles by providing incentives for buying hybrid and electric cars, making buildings more energy efficient, and building nuclear reactors.

India: India is also taking measures to reduce carbon dioxide emissions and has set targets such that the country's electricity would come from non-fossil fuel–based sources, such as wind and power, by 2030.

In general, nations around the globe are taking measures to develop a carbon-neutral future.

Automation and Digitalization[8, 9, 10]

From automotive to industrial and healthcare, automation/digitalization is the biggest trend shaping the future. *Digitalization* is the use of digital technologies to change a business model and provide new revenue and value-producing opportunities; it is the process of moving to a digital business. Key drivers are AI, machine learning, IoT, robotics, low-cost data processing, advanced sensors, voice recognition, augmented reality, and more. The pace of adoption has been rapid, in both manufacturing and service.

Robots are not new but with improvements and rapid changes in technologies such as motion sensors, machine vision, image and voice recognition, robots are able to perform increasingly sophisticated and delicate knowledge-based work. Advanced sensing technologies to provide comfort, safety, process automation, real-time data, and accuracy measurement are key enablers in automation. Sensors support a variety of applications, from providing security to measuring health-related data. In transportation, autonomous vehicles (AVs) have the potential to transform mobility and society as AVs are predicted to reduce traffic incidents and associated fatalities and injuries while also offering further environmental improvements.

Summary

- The world population is expected to reach 10.8 billion in 2050 from 7.7 billion in 2019. Shifts in economic power by 2050 will affect manufacturing and demand footprints.

- From automotive to industrial and healthcare, automation/digitalization is the biggest trend shaping the future. Companies of all sizes globally are leveraging digital technologies to drive value. COVID-19 has further boosted digitalization and the development of smart products and services.
- In emerging economies, there will be a significant demand for low-cost versions of products such as diapers, feminine hygiene products, sporting goods, medical equipment, vehicles, and more. Average salaries in these populations are less than $10,000.[11, 12, 13]
- Mobile and internet usage are transforming people's lives and the demand for equipment and devices has soared and will continue to grow.
- The world will need more than 70% energy by 2050 as compared to 2019 and the focus of innovation efforts is moving away from fossil fuels to alternative energy sources such as renewable energy and battery technology.
- China, the United States, India, and the European Union are the top countries emitting the highest amounts of carbon dioxide. As a result of climate change, there is a big shift driving the development of fuel-efficient vehicles, energy-efficient homes, pollution-free chemical plants, and the utilization of green and sustainable chemicals/products.

Build Your Roadmap[14]

As you think about your company's growth strategy, this model recommends that you consider the following dimensions:

- **Geographic:** Where do you manufacture products? Where are you selling? What regulations will impact your company? (i.e. emissions control). What are your best opportunities for global expansion? (i.e. low-cost products for emerging markets).
- **Corporate "white space":** Internet-based technologies are soaring – where might your company have competitive advantage (i.e. which applications/needs align with your core strengths?) What other megatrends signal new opportunities and emerging technologies for your company? Are there opportunities for your company to automate and increase efficiency? How can you leverage digitization, including AI, machine learning, and data analytics to uncover customer insights and opportunities?
- **Market shifts:** COVID-19 has created enormous opportunities – as well as challenges –which span the entire healthcare spectrum, from testing kits, to personal protection equipment, vaccines, and the way healthcare is delivered. The rise in telemedicine and virtual

appointments has opened markets and opportunities that could ultimately overtake traditional healthcare models. Healthcare is no longer limited to healthcare or medical device companies. The wellness trend opens the door for consumer products, food & beverage, appliance manufacturers, home building/construction. and more. How can you best serve the aging population? What other population trends might change your target market or impact your current customer base?

Once you have answered these questions, we suggest using this process[15] to narrow your focus:

- **Identify** potential areas of interest aligned with megatrends, strategic direction, and new emerging technology areas that complement your current business units.
- **Filter** by fit to your company's long-term vision and mission.
- **Further filter** by market potential and market timing. Invest in markets with significant potential but avoid investing in areas that are still "research stage." Conversely, avoid investing in markets where the opportunity has already been captured.

Megatrends combined with your own customer insight and analysis is a powerful guide to future planning. Technologies and external factors present opportunities (and threats) but ultimately your decisions should be market driven. The process outlined above will help you identify market segments where your company has strategic advantage as well as the right to play and the ability to win.

Reference

1. Lucintel publication, Assessing the Impact of COVID-19 on Various Industries, 2020.
2. Lucintel publication, IoT connectivity market Size, Forecast, Demand Trends, Competitive Analysis report – Lucintel, 2021.
3. Lucintel publication, Battery Materials Market Report: Trends, Forecast and Competitive Analysis, 2021.
4. Lucintel publication, Trends, Opportunities and Competitive Analysis of the Automated 3D Printing Market, 2021.
5. Lucintel publication, Five Trends Shaping the Future of the Artificial Intelligence Market, 2021.
6. Lucintel Publication, Growth Opportunities in Medical Device Market, 2020.
7. Lucintel publication, Opportunities in the Solar Photovoltaic Glass market: Market size, Trends and Growth Analysis, 2021.
8. Lucintel publication, Opportunities in the Sensor Market: Growth Trends, Forecast and Competitive Analysis, 2020.

9. Lucintel publication, Automotive Voice Recognition System Market: Trends, Forecast and Competitive Analysis, 2021.
10. Lucintel publication, Opportunities in the Augmented Reality and Virtual Reality Market: Growth Trends, Forecast and Competitive Analysis, 2021.
11. Lucintel publication, Opportunities and Competitive Analysis of the Baby Diaper Market, 2021.
12. Lucintel publication, Opportunities for the Feminine Hygiene Market in United States, 2021.
13. Lucintel publication, Opportunities in the Medical Equipment Maintenance Market: Market size, Trends and Growth Analysis, 2021.
14. **Innovation**edge, LLC., Build Your Roadmap ©
15. How Megatrends inform HP's investment strategies, Andrew Bolwell, May 24, 2018.

Section II

Identifying Opportunities, Partners, and Resources – Emerging Innovations by Selected Industries[1]

This section provides an in-depth analysis across seven industries selected either based upon their close ties to the megatrends (electronics, Internet of Things, and medical devices) or because of their historical proliferation of innovations applicable across multiple industries (automotive, aerospace, building construction, and chemical). Each chapter focuses on a single industry to facilitate opportunity/technology scouting, partner/resource selection, competitive intelligence gathering, and return on investment (ROI) estimation. Chapters are organized as follows:

1. **Emerging Innovations:** new technologies driving current and future innovation – descriptions, trends, highlights.
2. **Revenue Impact and Resulting Growth Opportunities:** innovations offering the highest future growth rates and largest current opportunities, including current and future market size, CAGR, and technology maturity. COVID impact is noted.
3. **Horizon Mapping Implications:** opportunities offering H2 and H3 potential for breakthrough innovation, long-term growth, and expansion beyond the core. COVID-19 has accelerated Horizon timetables though the definitions remain the same.

Use this section to identify attractive innovations, both in your target industry and in other industries. (Note that existing technologies transferred to new applications have led to many successful innovations!) Select the three to five most promising innovations and assess their growth and revenue potential as well as synergistic fit. Identify potential partners who offer these attractive innovations. Filter further to create a short list.

---

1 The selected industries are either closely related to megatrends or have historically been prolific in developing innovations applicable across multiple industries.

DOI: 10.4324/9781003177906-8

Chapter 5

Aerospace

In this chapter, we consider the following aspects of the aerospace industry:

- Emerging Innovations
- Revenue Impact and Resulting Growth Opportunities
- Horizon Planning Implications

Emerging Innovations

The aerospace industry is widely seen as the initiator of technology changes including the use of new metals, composites and plastics, advanced manufacturing processes, safety and security, and the development of more efficient and sustainable power and energy systems. In the aerospace industry, high customer expectations, stringent governmental regulations, increased competition, and the need for more fuel efficiency have been instrumental factors for technological developments.

Keeping aside the impact of corona virus on the aerospace industry, we will see significant research in advanced manufacturing processes such as 3D printing[1] and robotics. Spare parts that need to be replaced on a regular basis (such as door handles) and tools that are used to create aircraft parts will increasingly be 3D printed. Bob Smith, Chief Technology Officer of Honeywell Aerospace, is optimistic about new manufacturing methods, particularly 3D printing, which offer radical ways to design aircraft and components. He said, "Through 3D printing, we can actually make the strength where required and take out all the other weight."[2] Russ Dunn, Senior Vice President of GKN, also echoed on the use of revolutionary technologies for aircraft parts and said, "The combination of new technology and materials will revolutionize aircraft design and the way passengers travel. By 2050, 16 bn air passengers may be enjoying a radically different experience."[2]

Our observation is that industry players, in addition to improving their advanced manufacturing techniques, are focusing on the development of advanced inspection and safety features including electric de-icing systems[3], advanced communication systems, and more comprehensive

DOI: 10.4324/9781003177906-9

software to help pilots avoid accidents. For example, Johann Bordais, Vice President of Embraer Commercial Aviation Ltd., said

> By replacing traditional inspection procedures like general and detailed visual inspections and non-destructive inspections (X-ray, eddy current, and dye penetrant), less time would be needed to perform time-consuming disassembles to gain access to inspection areas. The inspection times would come down to minutes instead of hours in some cases.[4]

Anyone who takes commercial flights on even an irregular basis can clearly see that advancements in in-flight entertainment, safety features, health monitoring, and cleaning are creating new opportunities. For example, Boeing has developed a self-cleaning lavatory which uses ultraviolet light to kill germs after every use.

To summarize, we've assigned the top innovation opportunities[5] of the aerospace industry to the following broad categories (Figures 5.1 and 5.2).

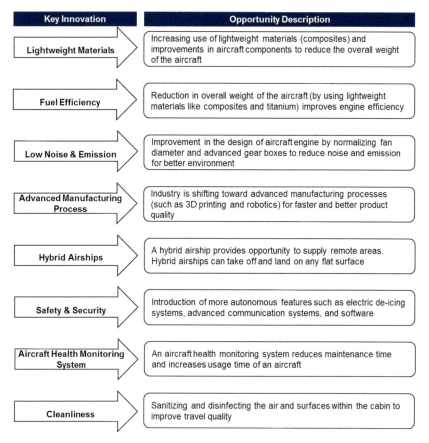

Figure 5.1 Key Innovation Areas for the Aerospace Industry.
Source: Lucintel.

Aerospace 53

Figure 5.2 Emerging Innovations in the Aerospace Industry. (a) Fuel and Noise Efficient Aero Engine; (b) 3D Printing of Turbine Wheel; (c) Hybrid Airship; (d) Self-Cleaning Lavatory.

The aerospace industry is conscious of its environmental impact and contribution to climate change. Strictly enforced rules and regulations have been made to control harmful emissions like CO_2 and NO_x. There are also rules for noise emission by aircraft. The aviation industry is spending resources on finding new solutions for noise and emission reduction such as the development of aircraft engines with innovative designs featuring improved gear boxes, increase of normalized fan diameter, and the usage of sound insulation. Original equipment manufacturers (OEMs) are also looking into electric aircraft to control emissions. "The European Union's Flightpath 2050 strategy" has set targets for CO_2 emissions in aviation to be reduced by 75% and noise by 65% by 2050 compared to the year 2000. Tom Enders, CEO of Airbus, said:

> At Airbus, our hybrid technology has been spurred by the European emission rules requiring that aircraft emit 75% less CO2 and generate 65% less noise in 2050 than in 2000. The ultimate goal for Airbus is to develop zero-emission aviation.[6]

Lightweight materials used in next-generation aircraft are gaining prominence as they curtail fuel consumption and emission levels necessary for regulatory compliance. For this reason, efforts to implement lightweight parts in aircraft have increased significantly. Geoff Hunt, Chief Engineer of UTC Aerospace Systems, said, "Titanium alloys have reduced the weight of landing gear by thousands of kilograms on the biggest jets."[2] Similarly, by making fan blades and the fan case from carbon fiber composites Rolls-Royce has been able to save 340 kg in engine weight.

Revenue Impact and Resulting Growth Opportunities

Our analysis suggests that innovation in **advanced manufacturing processes will offer the highest growth rate** during the forecast period, whereas innovation in **aero engines is the largest current opportunity** in which companies have significantly invested to drive the technology to maturity. Key drivers of advanced manufacturing processes are efficient use of raw materials, dimensional accuracy of final parts, customizable product creation, and error reduction while manufacturing parts. Companies can realize significant opportunities in advanced manufacturing processes, hybrid airships, aircraft health monitoring systems, and safety and security by investing in scaled-up capabilities and building technology platforms.

There is no doubt that growth opportunities in these areas will be slowed down in the short term due to the impact of COVID-19, since the commercial airline industry had almost stopped functioning during summer 2020 due to restrictions on travel. Interviews with major OEMs, such as Boeing and Airbus, suggest a decline of 20%–30% in the overall industry revenue in 2020 as compared to 2019 due to COVID-19. Boeing CEO Dave Calhoun said in April 27, 2020, that "It will take two to three years for travel to return to 2019 levels and an additional few years beyond that for the industry's long-term growth trend to return." When the turmoil in the airline industry does stabilize, he said "the commercial market will be smaller, and our customers' needs will be different."[7]

Table 5.1 shows the market size and growth rate for key innovation opportunity areas.

Lightweight materials, aero engine, and safety & security are the innovation areas in which aircraft component manufactueres and OEMs are investing for growth. Interestingly, innovation in aircraft engines offers an excellent opportunity though this segment is highly mature. Lightweight materials, of course, offer considerable opportunity and have the advantage of a medium degree of technological maturity, allowing for implementation across a wide range of platforms. Advanced manufacturing processes and safety & security provide fewer innovation opportunities but greater scope for commercial success.

Specifically, here's an overview of relative ease of commercialization and market potential for key innovation areas (Figure 5.3).

Table 5.1 Innovation Opportunities in the Aerospace Industry

Area of Innovation	Market Size (2019) (in $ Billion)	CAGR (2019–2035) (%)	Market Opportunity
Aircraft materials/ lightweight materials	7.6	6	• Composites • Titanium • Super alloys • Aluminum
Aero engines	72.8	4	• Advanced aircraft engines for low noise and emission
Advanced manufacturing processes	0.7	20	• 3D printing • Robotics
Hybrid airships	0.6	9	• Low-cost hybrid airships
Safety & security	26.8	3	• Electric de-icing • Advanced software • Advanced communication systems
Aircraft health monitoring systems	4.0	7	• Advanced sensors • Advanced predictive software

Source: Lucintel

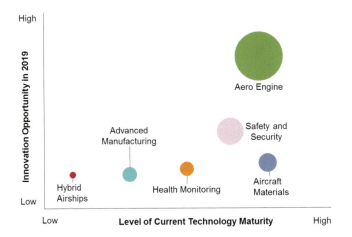

Figure 5.3 Level of Technology Maturity by Innovation Category in the Aerospace Industry.
Note: Size of the Bubble Represents Market Size in 2035.
Source: Lucintel.

The aero engine offers considerable opportunity and is highly mature. When the industry reaches a high level of maturity, the rate of innovation dwindles for product and process because companies are focused on cost, volume, and capacity. The areas of safety and security and aircraft health monitoring systems provide fewer innovation opportunities, but greater scope for commercial success. For those looking even further into the future, the landscapes for advanced manufacturing processes and hybrid airships offer fertile ground for innovation opportunities, but are still in the early days of the innovation curve.

Highlights

Below are some highlights of technological developments by industry players in the value chain of the aerospace industry in selected key innovation areas.

Fuel Efficiency: GE Aviation, Rolls-Royce, Pratt & Whitney, CFM International, and GKN Aerospace are developing technologies to manufacture fuel-efficient engines. GE Aviation developed the GenX-1B engine and Rolls-Royce developed the Trent 1000 engine, which consumes 15% less fuel in comparison to legacy engines. The GenX-1B engine has blades made with advanced material (TiAl). CFM International used CMC material for manufacturing shrouds and vanes for the F135. Pratt & Whitney has successfully tested next-generation Geared Turbofan (GTF) engine propulsion technology, an innovation that delivers 16% better fuel efficiency.

Lightweight Materials[8, 9, 10]: OEMs, Tier 1, Tier 2, and material suppliers are investing heavily in reducing the weight of aircraft parts. Boeing's use of composites in the B787 reduced weight and the number of parts in both the structure and the engine. **Airbus** uses advanced lightweight materials such as composites, titanium, and super alloys in the A350XWB's aircraft structure and engine.

Advanced Manufacturing: In the area of 3D printing, **Stratasys Ltd., The ExOne Company, and Arcam AB** are developing advanced manufacturing processes. Stratasys Ltd. has developed 3D printing parts for Boeing and Airbus. Engine and cabin interior components are typical applications for 3D printing.

Safety & Security[11]: Of course, safety and security is one of the major concerns in the aerospace industry. Companies such as **Airbus, Boeing, VT Miltope, and Altran** are developing stronger security cockpit doors. VT Miltope is developing security software for wireless cabin networks.

Aircraft Health Monitoring: In aircraft health monitoring, **Boeing and Tech Mahindra Boeing** are working with technologies like cloud computing, the Internet of Things (IoT), and big data technologies. These perform deep analytics related to an aircraft's health status and are instrumental in monitoring an airplane's state of wellbeing.

Cleanliness: Striding forward in the area of sanitation, **Boeing** is developing a flooring system that drains away moisture, leaving a dry, germ-free surface using heated floor panels; Boeing has also developed a prototype for a self-cleaning lavatory which kills germs by using UV light after every use. **Vilinger** is developing cabin floors with heated floor panels. Boeing is also developing a prototype for an innovative inspection robot specializing in the monitoring of confined spaces to ensure workers' safety and health, reducing risk in their working environment. **Recaro** is developing a self-cleaning business class seat that destroys virtually every germ by using a newly developed anti-bacterial film.

Due to COVID, airlines have taken significant measures to disinfect high-touch areas like arm rests, door handles, seat belts, tray tables, toilets, and flight decks. For example, United Airlines has started cleaning pilot flight decks since August 2020 with Ultraviolet C (UVC) lighting technology on most aircraft at its hub airports to disinfect the flight deck interior and continue providing pilots with a sanitary work environment. The airline is using hand-held AUVCo blades from the American Ultraviolet company to kill any viruses that may reside on sensitive switches and touch screen displays within the flight deck. American Airlines is using electrostatic spraying solution SurfaceWise®2 from Allied BioScience to clean surfaces inside its aircraft. The SurfaceWise2 solution is the first-ever long-lasting product to help fight the spread of the novel coronavirus that is approved by the US Environmental Protection Agency (EPA).

Horizon Planning Implications

To put these research findings in context, the chart below categorizes each opportunity area in terms of the Expanded Horizons Model[12] described in Chapter 1.

Definition of Each Innovation Type: Horizon 1 = Incremental, line extension, continuous improvement; **Horizon 2** = New to company or new to a sector; **Horizon 3** = Disruptive, new to the world (Table 5.2).

Table 5.2 Horizon Planning Implications for the Aerospace Industry

Area of Innovation	Horizon 1	Horizon 2	Horizon 3
Aero engine/fuel efficiency	Y	Y	
Lightweight materials	Y	Y	
Advanced manufacturing processes	Y	Y	Y
Hybrid airships		Y	Y
Safety & security	Y	Y	
Aircraft health monitoring systems	Y	Y	Y
Cleanliness	Y	Y	

Source: **Innovation**edge, LLC.
Content Source: Lucintel.

58 Emerging Innovations by Industry

Most of the opportunities can be categorized as Horizons 1 and 2, depending on strategy and investment. Trends and indicators would suggest the following approaches for those investing in the aerospace industry:

- **Aero Engines/Fuel Efficiency:** Given this area's high potential and projected growth rate, Horizon 1 and 2 opportunities are highly applicable. In particular, advances in engine technology and material innovations have the potential to create breakthrough products with customizable solutions that can suit a myriad of customers' needs. **Horizons 1 and/or 2 suitable.**
- **Lightweight Materials**[13, 14]: This category **has the largest growth opportunity** for game-changing materials such as CMC, composites, titanium aluminide, and nano-composites – materials that are highly regarded for their enormous weight-saving benefits. **Horizons 1 and/or 2 suggested.**
- **Advanced Manufacturing:** Within this category, promising technologies such as 3D printing and robotic manufacturing present Horizon 3 potential. **Horizon 3 suggested.**
- **Hybrid Airships:** In our estimation, this is one of the most disruptive areas of innovation, as it offers a broad, as yet untapped market opportunity. Within this category, promising technologies such as steerable, diesel-powered fans for propulsion and control, rudders, and ailerons present Horizon 3 potential. **Horizon 3 suggested.**
- **Safety and Security:** This area presents the most sizable current opportunity, making it suitable as a core or incremental activity. Safety features in aircraft are creating new market opportunities embraced by passengers, regulators, and providers in the areas of electric de-icing systems, advanced communication and infotainment systems, software, and alert systems for both pilots and passengers. **Horizons 1 and/or 2 suggested.**
- **Aircraft Health Monitoring:** Again, with an eye toward safety, expanding safety requirements and better defect detection techniques are creating an opportunity for aircraft health monitoring systems. This category is a solid, steady-as-she-goes industry with potential breakthroughs in digital displays, biological sensors in seats, retractable screens and trays, augmented-reality screens, and advanced alert systems. **Horizons 1, 2 or 3 suggested.**
- **Cleanliness:** Within this category, the cleanliness of confined spaces and the sanitation of seats, flight deck, and lavatories are three major areas for innovation and growth. Due to COVID, significant initiatives have been taken by airliners around the world to disinfect high-touch areas like arm rests, door handles, seat belts, tray tables, toilets, and flight decks. For example, United Airlines has started cleaning pilot flight decks with UVC lighting technology on most

aircrafts. American Airlines is using electrostatic spraying solution SurfaceWise®2 from Allied BioScience to clean surfaces inside its aircraft. **Horizons 1 and/or 2 suggested.**

All in all, it's quite clear that the seven key innovation areas in the aerospace industry hold good growth potential as the overall industry continues to expand. The megatrends of fuel efficiency, lightweight materials, advanced manufacturing, hybrid airships, safety and security, aircraft health monitoring, and cleanliness make this industry ripe for innovation both in the short term and in the long term.

References

1. Lucintel publication, Industrial 3D Printing Market Report: Trends, Forecast and Competitive Analysis, 2021.
2. Peggy Hollinger, "Airlines bid to beat their weight problem", *Financial Times*, Dec. 14, 2016.
3. Lucintel publication, Trends, Opportunities and Competitive Analysis of the Aerospace Electrical De-Icing System Market, 2020.
4. "Aircraft health monitoring sensors cutting MRO costs", *Aviation Week*, Aug. 12, 2016.
5. Lucintel publication, Innovation Trends Shaping the Aerospace Industry, 2021.
6. Alanna Petroff, "Airbus hopes to launch hybrid passenger planes by 2030", *CNN Business*, Apr. 07, 2016.
7. Leslie Josephs, "Boeing CEO says air travel recovery could take two to three years; board wins approval", *CNBC*, Apr. 27, 2020.
8. Lucintel publication, Composites in the Aerospace Market Report: Trends, Forecast and Competitive Analysis, 2020.
9. Lucintel publication, Titanium in the Global Aerospace Industry Report: Trends, Forecast and Competitive Analysis, 2021.
10. Lucintel publication, Opportunities in the Aircraft Engine Blade Market: Market size, Trends and Growth Analysis, 2020.
11. Lucintel publication, Opportunities in the Ballistic Protection Market: Growth Trends, Forecast and Competitive Analysis, 2021.
12. **Innovation**edge, LLC., Expanded Horizons Model ©
13. Lucintel publication, Growth Opportunities for Ceramic Matrix Composites in the Global Aerospace Industry, 2017.
14. Lucintel publication, Opportunities and Competitive Analysis of the Composites in the Aerospace Interior Market, 2020.

Chapter 6

Automotive

In this chapter, we consider the following aspects of the automotive industry:

- Emerging Innovations
- Revenue Impact and Resulting Growth Opportunities
- Horizon Planning Implications

Emerging Innovations

Innovation in the automotive industry is powered by new technology developments such as Advanced Driver Assistance Systems (ADAS), vehicle automation, and vehicle connectivity. **Electric vehicles (EVs), autonomous vehicles, and shared mobility services are creating new markets/applications** as well as a demand for replacements and upgrades as older technologies become obsolete.

Driver and passenger safety and comfort have always been paramount (anti-lock brakes, collision avoidance systems, radar detection, etc.), and original equipment manufacturers (OEMs) are now focusing on powertrain and telematics improvements. Mike Mansuetti, President of Bosch North America, stated

> As electrification goes main-stream, the powertrain advancement is evolving. We combine the electric motor, power electronics, and transmission into one compact unit called eAxle that directly drives the vehicle. Bosch is taking a two-pronged approach, and continuing to offer the expertise and knowledge on both electro-mobility and combustion engines.[1]

Ford is adding intuitive technology with advanced algorithms to predict where nearby vehicles, cyclists, and pedestrians might go, ensuring drivers see them in time. Mercedes-Benz is integrating cruise control with

DOI: 10.4324/9781003177906-10

a TomTom 3D mapping[2] system in its trucks to predict road undulations and adjust the course accordingly.

We have observed that in the past five to ten years, the automotive industry has increased advancement in four key technologies: **ADAS, Vehicle Automation, Vehicle Connectivity,** and **New Mobility Services.** In addition, regulatory pressure[3,4] on fuel economy, emissions, and safety requirements has accelerated advancement in materials and process innovation.

Carbon dioxide (CO_2) emission reduction is one of the biggest regulatory requirements globally – in Europe, for instance, CO_2 discharges of all models in one year need to drop from 140 g CO_2 per kilometer to 95 g by 2020 and to 75 g (or less) by 2025. All major OEMs are concentrating on using innovative lightweight materials and new techniques to meet these standards. BMW is significantly investing in lightweight technologies and utilizing aluminum and carbon composites to make vehicle parts. BMW is also using mix material technology and combining carbon fiber with steel and aluminum. According to the product manager of Volkswagen, weight and cost reduction are two factors where Volkswagen is focusing currently with compound materials. An expected weight reduction of 20% and cost reduction of 30% is possible with the improvement in the components.

As per our study, OEMs are also developing more electric/hybrid cars and stepping up battery innovation. Faster-charging, longer-range battery power innovations will contribute to 32EV adoption in the future; lithium-ion technology, which offers lighter weight and longer service life, will see impressive investments and further development. Mark Russ, president of GM, tells us that General Motors (GM) has decided to phase out manufacturing cars that rely on diesel and gasoline and move toward an all-electric, zero emission product line in the future. GM believes in an all-electric future. GM is committed to driving increased usage and acceptance of EVs through no-compromise solutions that meet their customer needs.[5]

Most vehicles are expected to be self-driving by 2030 and OEMs are currently road testing autonomous cars. GM is testing the Super Cruise, which controls the vehicle on long highways with minimal driver assistance, and California's department of motor vehicles has issued permits to Google, Tesla, Volkswagen, Mercedes-Benz, and several others to test self-driving cars on its state public roads. For example, GM is continuing to make great progress on its plans to commercialize autonomous vehicles. GM has already planned to deploy self-driving taxis in major cities. The company announced a major investment of $300 million in its Orion Township, Michigan, factory; one more line of self-driving cars will be added there. To cope with increasing competition in this market, Ford also announced an investment of $900 million in its Michigan plant in order to increase the production of autonomous cars.

To sum up, we have broadly categorized these innovation opportunities as follows (Figures 6.1 and 6.2).

Autonomous cars and **ADAS** are the most disruptive innovation areas in the global automotive industry and **powertrain advancement** offers the highest future growth rate during the forecast period. We are also noticing technological trends in gesture controls, biometric access and advanced display systems, reconfigurable cabins, and lighting. Bosch is working on the development of ADAS and automated driving. The company focuses on the functional development and derivation of requirements for

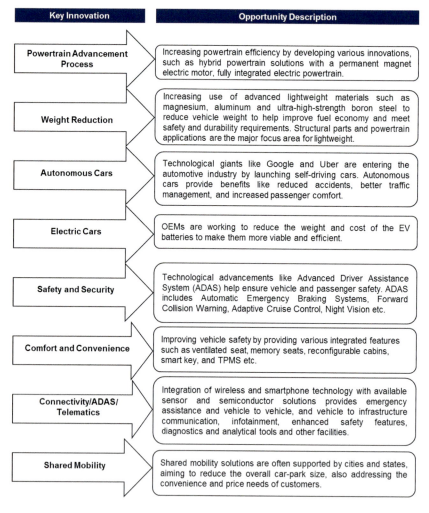

Figure 6.1 Key Areas of Innovation Opportunity for the Automotive Industry.
Source: Lucintel.

Automotive 63

Figure 6.2 Emerging Innovations in the Automotive Industry. (a) Autonomous Cars; (b) Electric Vehicles; (c) Car Airbags; (d) Advanced Driver Assistance Systems; (e) Connected Cars.

systems and products of automated driving, sensors, the vehicle architecture, actuators[6] and their integration into the vehicle. Frank Sgambati, director of product planning and innovation management at Bosch states, that the sensor technology developed by Bosch includes radar[7], video, and ultrasonic sensors[8]. Bosch is using prototype vehicles as a tool for the definition of sensor and system requirements.[9]

EVs, connected vehicles, and telematics along with improved **comfort, convenience, safety and security** features are the main innovation areas that manufacturers and component suppliers are investing in for growth. Jessica Cicchino, Vice President of Insurance institute for Highway Safety, brings to our knowledge that lane departure warning and blind spot detection systems help prevent crashes, which allows for future integration of additional features such as driver drowsiness warning, traffic sign recognition, and headlight control. The large number of fatal crashes that involve unintentional lane departures, technology aimed at preventing them has the potential to save a lot of lives.[10] In terms of passenger safety, we are noticing a significant increase in the number of airbags per car. As per the product development manager of Volvo,

> Airbags are fitted throughout the vehicle interiors, right from the steering wheel to dashboard to door panels, and seat frames. Emerging application of the airbags is sideways and exterior of the car to offer protection for pedestrians and traffic on the road. External airbags for car will offer safety to the people inside the car, as well as emphasize the safety of those on the road and the car itself. European carmakers have taken the lead in experimenting with external airbags in a bid to protect the pedestrians and cyclists in the event of in-head collision with cars.[11]

Revenue Impact and Resulting Growth Opportunities

Our analysis suggest that innovations in **autonomous vehicles, EVs, ADAS, connected cars, and shared mobility will be growing rapidly with double-digit growth** during the forecast period (2019–2035), while **powertrain offers the largest current opportunity** where the technology is mature. Growth drivers are the rapid progress in artificial intelligence, increasing innovation in software-based systems, technological developments in sensors, the development of a supportive regulatory framework, government funding, and investments in digital infrastructure.

There is no doubt that growth in these opportunities will be slowed down in the short term due to the impact of COVID-19. Major OEMs, such as GM and Ford, suggest a decline of 20%–30% in overall industry revenue based on decreased demand in 2020 due to COVID-19.

Once vaccines for coronavirus are developed and the economy becomes normal, we predict good growth for various innovative products and technologies in the automotive industry. Companies can realize significant opportunities in shared mobility, electric cars, autonomous cars, safety & security, and ADAS with the right strategy. Table 6.1 shows the market size and growth rate for key innovation opportunity areas.

Disruptive technologies can change the game for businesses, creating entirely new products and services, as well as shifting pools of value between producers or from producers to consumers. Organizations may need new business models to capture some of that value.

In terms of the **degree of disruption**, development of **autonomous cars, ADAS, shared mobility, and connected cars** offer the most significant opportunities. These areas of innovation would disrupt automotive, electronics, business service, and insurance services, and are expected to

Table 6.1 Innovation Opportunities in the Automotive Industry

Area of Innovation	Market Size (2019) (in $ Billion)	CAGR (2019–2035) (%)	Market Opportunity
Lightweight materials market	78	3.6	• Advanced high-strength steel • Aluminum • Glass and carbon fiber-based composites
Connected cars	62	15.4	• Low-emission ICE
EV	93	16.2	• Low-cost hybrid systems
Autonomous cars	7	28.7	• Increasing innovations in software-based systems • Rapid progress in artificial intelligence
ADAS	18	18.8	• High demand for user-friendly interface for digitization of driver and passenger experiences
Safety and security	100	9.8	• Development of features, such as AEBS, FCW, ACC
Comfort and convenience	7.8	24.5	• Improving vehicle comfort and convenience features, such as ventilated seat, memory seats
Powertrain	565	2.8	• Development of hybrid engines • Increasing use of alternative fuels
Shared mobility	84	3.1	• Consumer online platform providers offer solutions
Vehicle telematics	36	25.5	• Vehicle tracking in commercial vehicles

Source: Lucintel

change supply chains. Autonomous cars are expected to reduce the demand for personal cars. To offset losses, car companies and dealerships will have to invest in new products, such as car-sharing services or car fleet management. Some of the companies who are taking a lead role in this space are Google, Tesla, GM, and Volkswagen.

As for the **size of innovation, electric cars** and **autonomous cars** top the list. Key factors are environmental concerns, stringent government rules, and advances in battery technology, high oil prices, and the desire to reduce greenhouse gas emissions. Ford Motors, GM, Volkswagen, and Toyota Motors are heavily investing in autonomous car and electric car technology, while auto suppliers such as Magna International, ZF TRW, Denso Corporation, Faurecia, Lear, Adient, Bosch, and Continental AG are focusing on the R&D and technology commercialization of ADAS and other safety & security features.

Innovation in powertrains offers a large opportunity, while innovation in autonomous cars, EVs, ADAS, and shared mobility offers a lower degree of technological maturity. Safety & security and comfort and convenience provide moderate innovation opportunities but greater scope for commercialization success.

Though innovation and disruption potential are great, the automotive industry faces numerous compliance requirements from the government and its own internal standards of excellence. Such requirements cover aspects of the supply chain and include materials usage, counterfeit parts, manufacturing procedures, and more.

Every year the automotive industry rolls out the latest and greatest vehicles and concept cars at auto shows around the globe in a bid to capture consumers' interest. Car companies, inventors, and others have been demonstrating innovations for years – often touting "revolutionary" design and technology.

In the past, OEMs and parts suppliers focused on engine power and size, gearbox, and vehicle design, while today most are focusing on powertrain advancement, autonomous cars, electric cars, ADAS, and comfort and convenience. Enablers include rapid growth and advances in artificial intelligence, software, robotics/HMI features, GPS, navigation devices, and other intelligence and connectivity features.

Many innovation projects involve large R&D expenditure. Studies say that only 20% of the total R&D expenditure will result in strong return on investment (ROI), and only 10% of new innovations have blockbuster potential. While these odds may be true in any industry, companies need to carefully assess the potential and risks of specific projects, choosing those aligned with internal strengths and capabilities. It is also important to weigh the risk of falling behind.

Specifically, here's an overview of the level of current technology maturity and market potential for key innovation areas (Figure 6.3).

Powertrain offers the largest opportunity and is highly commercialized. Innovation in lightweight materials offers a lower degree of disruption within a wide range of platforms. Safety & security and comfort and convenience offer fewer innovation opportunities but greater scope for commercial success (e.g. automatic emergency braking system (AEBS), forward collision warning (FCW), adaptive cruise control (ACC), ventilated seat, memory seats, reconfigurable cabins, smart key, sunroof, and ambient lighting). Autonomous cars, EVs, ADAS, and shared mobility are in the early stages of the innovation curve. The future potential is high.

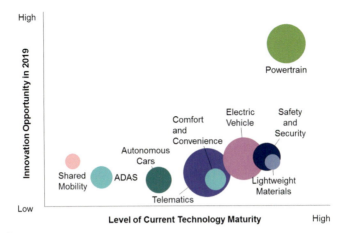

Figure 6.3 Level of Technology Maturity by Innovation Category in the Global Automotive Industry.
Note: Size of the Bubble Represents Market Size in 2035.
Source: Lucintel.

Highlights

Autonomous Cars[12, 13]: Companies such as **Tesla, Google, GM, and Volkswagen** are developing disruptive technologies to deliver autonomous cars. Google is focusing on fully autonomous vehicles with small-scale deployment of low-speed L5 self-driving vehicles for campus-like environments and cities. GM announced the expenditure of $100 million to begin production of its self-driving electric Chevy Bolt while Volkswagen launched Sedric with full "Level 5" autonomy.

Electric Vehicle[14, 15]: EV and battery innovation is coming from companies such as Tesla, GM, Nissan, and others. Tesla launched its Model 3 small electric car with a battery that achieves 220 miles of range. Chevrolet launched the hybrid electric car Volt with 420 miles on a full charge.

Volvo announced that it is phasing out internal combustion engines (ICEs) beginning in 2019 and will begin selling electric trucks in Europe in 2019. Ford announced that it is investing $11 billion in EVs and plans to bring 24 hybrid and 16 fully electric cars to market by 2022. GM announced its plan to bring 20 fully electric models to market by 2023.

Weight Reduction[16, 17]: **Ford, Toyota, BMW, Volkswagen,** and other OEMs are increasing the usage of lightweight materials, such as aluminum, AHSS, composites, and titanium. Ford Motors aims to reduce 250–750 lbs weight per vehicle, while Toyota Motors plans to reduce vehicle weight by 10%–30% for mid-sized vehicles.

68 Emerging Innovations by Industry

Powertrain Advancement[18]**: ZF TRW, GKN Plc, and BorgWarner** are developing advanced electric drives and the hybridization of transmission technology suitable for fully electric or hybrid applications.

Safety and Security[19, 20]**: Robert Bosch, Delphi Automotive,** and other suppliers are innovating better driving experiences that include safety technologies such as heads-up display (HUD), anti-lock braking systems (ABS), electronic stability control (ESC), tire pressure monitoring system (TPMS) airbag, seatbelts. Innovations in ADAS will improve driver enjoyment.

Comfort and Convenience[21, 22]**: Companies such as **Faurecia, Lear, and Adient** are working on innovations. Faurecia developed an active wellness seat for driver and passenger comfort. Lear and Adient launched ventilated seats and memory seats.

Horizon Planning Implications

To put these research findings in context, the chart below categorizes each opportunity area in terms of the Expanded Horizons Model[23] described in Chapter 1.

Definition of Each Innovation Type: Horizon 1 = Incremental, line extension, continuous improvement; **Horizon 2** = New to company or new to a sector, **Horizon 3** = Disruptive, new to the world (Table 6.2).

Most of the opportunities can be categorized as Horizons 1 and 2. Trends and indicators would suggest the following approach for those investing in the automotive industry:

- **Weight reduction:** This area has the largest current opportunity as well as technological maturity, making it suitable as a core or incremental activity. **Horizons 1 and/or 2 are suitable,** though identifying untapped customer needs could lead to H3 endeavors. In particular, advances in manufacturing technology and material innovations

Table 6.2 Horizon Planning Implications for the Automotive Industry

Area of Innovation	Horizon I	Horizon 2	Horizon 3
Weight reduction	Y	Y	
Fuel efficiency	Y	Y	
Powertrain advancement	Y	Y	Y
Safety & security	Y	Y	
Comfort & convenient	Y	Y	
Electric cars	Y	Y	Y
Autonomous cars	Y	Y	Y
Connectivity/ADAS/telematics	Y	Y	Y
Shared mobility	Y	Y	Y

Source: **Innovation**edge, LLC.
Content Source: Lucintel

have the potential for creating breakthrough products such as carbon fiber technology, advances in nanotechnology and 3D printing. **Horizon 3 suggested.**

- **Powertrain Advancement:** This category can be a launchpad for a game-changing electric and hybrid propulsion system that will lead the future of mobility. **Horizon 1, 2, or 3 suggested.**
- **Safety and Security/Comfort & Convenience:** This area has the largest current opportunity, making it suitable as a core or incremental activity. Along with airbags, seatbelts, and whiplash protection systems, the ability to detect, monitor, and prevent serious consequences in real time is becoming a must for all vehicles. **Horizons 1 and/or 2 are suitable,** though identifying untapped customer needs could lead to H3 endeavors.
- **Autonomous and Electric Cars:** Within this category, promising technologies such as **advance powertrain, battery innovation,** and **level 5 autonomous car** present Horizon 3 potential. **Horizon 1, 2, or 3 suggested.**
- **ADAS**[24]**:** Along with automatic emergency braking system (AEBS), ACC, parking assistance system (PAS), and night vision (NV) systems, the ability to detect, monitor, and control vehicle threat in real time is becoming mandatory. This category is a solid one with potential breakthroughs in advanced grid systems, AEBS, FCW systems, ACC, blind spot detection (BSD), lane departure warning (LDW), PAS, pedestrian detection system (PDS), traffic sign recognition (TSR), NV system, driver drowsiness detection (DDD). **Horizon 1, 2, or 3 suggested.**
- **Shared Mobility**[25]**:** Within this category, car and bike sharing along with ride hailing services are already prevalent and show no signs of slowing down. **Horizon 1, 2, or 3 suggested.**

The nine key opportunity areas in the automotive industry all hold high growth potential as the overall industry continues to expand. The trends in automotive production, emphasis on driver and passenger comfort & safety, fuel efficiency/emission trends, and driverless cars combined with electric powertrain technology development make this industry ripe for innovation both in the short and in the long term.

References

1. "Detroit Auto Show – NAIAS 2018", *Bosch*, Jan. 16, 2018.
2. Lucintel publication, Opportunities in the Automotive In-Dash Navigation System Market: Market size, Trends and Growth Analysis, 2021.
3. Lucintel publication, Growth Opportunities in the Global Automotive Fuel Tank Market, 2021.
4. Lucintel publication, Low Emission Vehicle: Trends, Forecast and Competitive Analysis, 2021.

5. Paul A. Eisenstein, "GM is going all electric, will ditch gas- and diesel-powered cars", *NBC News*, Oct. 03, 2017.
6. Lucintel publication, Trends, Opportunities and Competitive Analysis of the Automotive Actuator Market, 2021.
7. Lucintel publication, Opportunities in the Automotive Radar Market: Growth Trends, Forecast and Competitive Analysis, 2021.
8. Lucintel publication, Opportunities and Competitive Analysis of the Automotive Ultrasonic Sensor Market, 2021.
9. Tom. Murphy, "Bosch puts autonomous tech in park", *Wards Auto*, Jun. 06, 2016.
10. "Lane departure warning, blind spot detection help drivers avoid trouble", *Automotive World*, Aug. 23, 2017.
11. Noah Joseph, "Your next car could have airbags on the outside", *Autoblog*, Feb. 14, 2016.
12. Lucintel publication, Trends, Opportunities and Competitive Analysis of the Automotive HMI (Human Machine Interface) Market, 2020.
13. Lucintel publication, Opportunities and Competitive Analysis of the Self-Driving Bus Market, 2021.
14. Lucintel publication, Opportunities in the Electric Vehicle Market: Growth Trends, Forecast and Competitive Analysis, 2021.
15. Lucintel Publication, Trends, Opportunities and Competitive Analysis of the Connected Car Market, 2021.
16. Lucintel publication, Growth Opportunities in the Global Automotive Lightweight Materials Market, 2020.
17. Lucintel publication, Opportunities in the Automotive Aluminum Market: Growth Trends, Forecast and Competitive Analysis, 2020.
18. Lucintel publication, Growth Opportunities in the Global Electric Vehicle Powertrain Market, 2021.
19. Lucintel publication, Growth Opportunities in the Global Automotive ADAS Market, 2017.
20. Lucintel publication, Opportunities in the Automotive Biometric Market: Market size, Trends and Growth Analysis, 2021.
21. Lucintel publication, Automotive Ambient Lighting Market Report: Trends, Forecast and Competitive Analysis, 2020.
22. Lucintel publication, Opportunities in the Automotive Ventilated Seat Market: Market size, Trends and Growth Analysis, 2020.
23. **Innovation**edge, LLC., Expanded Horizons Model ©
24. Lucintel publication, Opportunities and Competitive Analysis of the Automotive Artificial Intelligence Market, 2021.
25. Lucintel publication, Shared Mobility Market Report: Trends, Forecast and Competitive Analysis , 2021.

Chapter 7

Chemical

In this chapter, we consider the following aspects of the chemical industry:

– Emerging Innovations
– Revenue Impact and Resulting Growth Opportunities
– Horizon Planning Implications

Emerging Innovations

Though the chemical industry is relatively mature, our study suggests that there are significant areas for growth and innovation. Major players are shifting their focus from commodity-based chemicals to specialized chemicals such as **functional materials, green coatings, self-healing powder coating, biodegradable polymers,** and **nano-pesticides** to improve profitability and differentiation.

We have observed that the chemical industry is diverse with a plethora of products that are not necessarily visible to consumers yet are essential components of products they use. Many products are also intermediates, produced for and sold to other chemical companies. Raw materials are converted into more than 70,000 different products such as polymers, rubber, pigments, paints, coatings, adhesives, fibers, textiles, fertilizers, pesticides, and more. This chapter focuses on innovations in three major areas of the chemical industry:

1. Paints and coatings
2. Polymers, and
3. Agrochemicals

One of the key innovation drivers is environmental responsibility as companies seek to create chemicals that are more sustainable and cost-effective. CEO and Chairman of AkzoNobel, Thierry Vanlancker, tells that they particularly emphasize on increasing their energy efficiency

DOI: 10.4324/9781003177906-11

and reducing material waste and continue to deliver more eco-premium solutions and water-based products to their customers. Further, he adds:

> Sustainability is clearly good for business. Relevant cutting-edge innovation is also a key to delivering on our strategy and we are making great progress with our sustainable product development, especially in terms of providing customers with more sustainable solutions and greater functionality.[1]

Green coating, biodegradable polymers, and **biofuel coatings** manufactured from renewable resources are among the most innovative areas[2, 3]. Mr. Ken Richards from Leaf Resources also said:

> In packaging market, there is a strong and growing consumer preference towards biodegradable materials because of environmental concerns. There has therefore been a concentrated focus in recent years on developing new barrier coating technology that is either renewably sourced, readily recyclable, biodegradable or all three.[4]

In **agrochemicals, nanotechnology is** reducing the toxic impact of chemical pesticides and providing target-specific control of crop pests by developing nano-pesticides.

Regulations to reduce energy consumption and VOC (volatile organic compound) emissions by using bio-based resin create both opportunities and challenges. Bioresin in UV coating is transitioning from solvent-borne to water-borne, which has been at the core of sustainability efforts by the coatings industry. Susan Kendall, Sustainability Director at AkzoNobel Decorative Paints, is confident that their customers want to create spaces that are energy efficient, and this has pushed them to create an innovative range of coatings that are easy to apply and independently tested. She also says that increasing energy prices are placing a greater burden on everyone, including private, residential, and commercial customers. The majority of energy consumption comes from heating and cooling: approximately two-thirds in the average home and half in the average commercial building.[5]

We will now be discussing innovation opportunities in coating, polymers, and agrochemicals.

Emerging Innovations in Coatings

In coatings, there are many areas which are driving innovations in terms of environmental-friendly coating or functional coating or self-healing coating or a better value proposition. For better understanding, we have

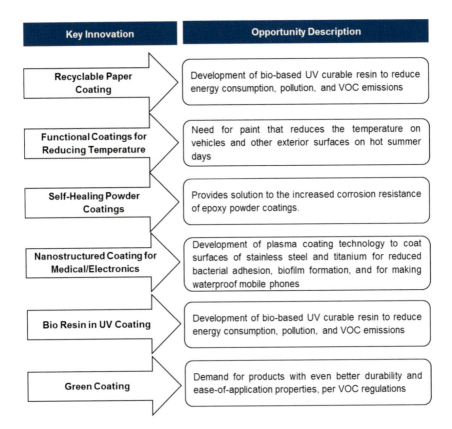

Figure 7.1 Key Innovation Areas for the Coatings Market.
Source: Lucintel.

provided a broad categorization of the top innovation opportunities in the coatings market as below (Figure 7.1).

As per our analysis, **recyclable paper coating** is a revolutionary new water-based treatment that will survive multi-directional scores, folds, and creases without surrendering its barrier properties. Paperboards treated with recyclable paper coatings provide an excellent barrier to water, oil, and grease. Dow Paper Coatings has seen a shift toward a heightened interest in compostable and biodegradable paper products as stated by Bob Gargione, global business manager at Dow Paper Coatings. He further stated that the company has responded to the demand in the food packaging industry for technologies that improve the performance of paper and paperboard coatings with low binder levels.[6]

We find significant innovations in **functional coatings designed for temperature management which reflect infrared light to reduce heat** absorption, thus helping to **reduce energy consumption and significant power savings on air conditioning.** Functional paints can reduce the vehicle surface temperature by up to 20°C, thus cooling the interior.

Self-healing[7] is getting a lot of attention these days, whether it is for coatings or for plastics or for composites. The market for self-healing coating is forecast to grow at double digits and offers a promising future as they reduce costly maintenance burdens and improve safety in construction, electronics, consumer products, oil and gas, wind energy, military, automotive, and aerospace industries. Truong, Physical Scientist at the US Army Natick Soldier Research Center, says:

> The self-healing coatings can be a spray-on coating or a continuous coating – depending on the type of protective clothing they are applied on. The idea is just like when a scratch breaks open the skin. Our body has the ability to heal and mend, make a scab and heal. A coating that can automatically heal itself could prove beneficial by automatic recovering properties (such as mechanical, electrical and aesthetic properties), and thus extending the lifetime of the coating.[8]

Another great area for growth in the coating market is in the development of **nanostructured coatings** for medical device and electronics. Dr. Yugen Zhang from the Institute of Bioengineering and Nanotechnology (IBN) says,

> Nano coating is designed to disinfect surfaces in a novel yet practical way. There is an urgent need to disinfect medical devices/surfaces without causing any harm to the environment. Nano-coating will help us to prevent the transmission of infectious diseases from contact with medical devices or other surfaces.[9]

Superior performance capabilities coupled with increasing application of nano-coating in consumer electronics and healthcare are driving growth. Nanostructured coating is one of the largest innovative markets in coatings with a double-digit growth forecast (Figure 7.2).

We are also seeing significant development in **bio-based UV curable resins**[10] to **reduce energy consumption, pollution,** and **VOC emissions.** As stated by Jim Seefeld, MD of Cambridge Polymers:

> Bioresin is formaldehyde-free, removing the risk of exposure, providing benefits for environmental health and personal safety. Bioresin can bring savings through a reduced requirement for emission abatement on production lines. Bioresin provides a marketing advantage for products being environmentally friendly, sustainable and formaldehyde-free.[11]

Figure 7.2 Innovations in Nano-coatings Market. (a) Nano-Coatings for Electronics Device; (b) Nano-Coatings for Medical Implants.

Another innovation area is in the development of **green coatings** such as water-borne coatings[12], powder coatings, high-solid coatings, and radiation-cured coatings, which **emit extremely low or no VOCs**. As per our findings, green coatings offer the largest future market opportunity in the coatings market. Steve Revnew, Vice President, Product Development, Sherwin-Williams, states that

> Low VOC coatings have seen continued growth. The reason for this growth is two-fold. First, VOC regulations continue to become more stringent and second, more buildings are being built using green standards. Going green has become popular with professionals in the paint industry as well as with consumers across the board, and professionals are keeping up with the interest in green coatings from all perspectives, both by acknowledging the demand aspect as well as from the perspective of meeting regulations by specifying the appropriate product.[13]

Recent innovations include multi-purpose latex primer/sealer, industrial multi-surface acrylic coats, and water-based paints with easier clean-up and low odor.

Emerging Innovations in Polymers

There are many areas within polymers which are driving innovations in terms of better performance or better processing or for better value proposition. These innovations are replacing traditional materials. For better understanding, we have provided a broad categorization of the top innovation opportunities in the polymer market as below (Figure 7.3).

In adhesives, **light cure adhesive technology offers a breakthrough solution** over traditional curing technologies. Light cure adhesives

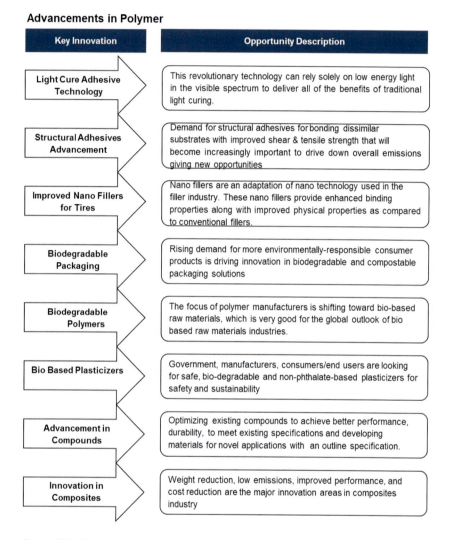

Figure 7.3 Key Innovation Areas for the Polymers Market.
Source: Lucintel.

exceed both industry and environmental standards, ensuring a safer working environment, reducing unnecessary energy usage, and saving replacement, maintenance, repair, and capital investment costs. Increasing demand for light cure adhesives in compact electronic devices and flexible packaging solutions are major growth drivers for this market (Figure 7.4).

Figure 7.4 UV Light Curing of Automotive Adhesive.

Advancements on structural adhesives[14] offer the **largest opportunity in the adhesives market**. Selamawit Belli from Dow Automotive Solutions is confident that structural adhesives will make a significant impact on the lives of hundreds of millions of new consumers. He further says that unlike new joining methods such as laser welding, you can actually deploy adhesives in the aftermarket as well. Using structural adhesives can cut factory spot welding by as much as 50%, cutting up to 22 pounds of metal from the mass of the vehicle. Perhaps even more importantly for original equipment manufacturers (OEMs), adhesives can join aluminum to steel cheaper and faster (50%–100% faster). They adhere well to substrates and can be applied quickly in a cost-effective manner.[15] Compilation of major applications of structural adhesives is provided in Figure 7.5.

Another market which is expected to experience high growth will be innovations in **nano-fillers**. Basically, nano-fillers are additives that consist of inorganic materials which enhance the mechanical and physical properties of the composites formed. The nano-filler demand for end-use applications is expected to increase owing to its ease of processing, sound absorption, advantageous mechanical and physical properties, and peripheral properties (such as flame retardancy). **Biodegradable packaging** products are also one of the areas with increasing adoption in a wide variety of industries, owing to their low environmental impact and growing demand for sustainable solutions. In particular, the food and beverage industry is using polymers extensively to promote green living and reduce waste. For example, BASF is concentrating particularly on developing whole systems; it is currently researching intensively on compostable hot drink lids for paper cups, and the cups are

Figure 7.5 Applications of Structural Adhesives in Various Industries. (a) Automotive; (b) Aerospace; (c) Marine; (d) Wind.

coated with biodegradable polymers instead of polyethylene, as told by Dr. Robert.[16] Governments are emphasizing bio-based materials with steps like ban on plastic carrier bags.

Along with biodegradable packaging, innovations in **bio-plasticizers can also help to reduce the carbon footprint**. James Stephenson from Geon Performance Materials states,

> The bio-plasticizers can capitalize the growing trend in the consumer market towards transparency of materials. Demand for the bio-plasticizer and its material is strong in North America, but demand also exists in Europe. Consumers want a phthalate-free alternative, and this technology is designed to deliver on that need.[17]

The demand for bio-plasticizers[18] is growing due to **stringent government regulations** and **rising consumer health concerns**. Increasing demand from developing countries coupled with manufacturers' preference for phthalate-free plasticizers are the prime growth drivers of this market.

We also found that innovations in **polymer compounds** will hold an impressive opportunity in the coming years. The plastic compounding business is boosted by the **growing consumption** from downstream industries such as automotive, building/construction, electrical/electronic, and packaging. Another growth area of innovations in polymer is in composites[19], which is allowing the use of polymers in a variety of industries for structural and semi-structural applications. Polymer composites are competing with steel and aluminum and offer light weight solutions in a trillion dollar structural materials market.

> Advanced thermoplastic composites are an emerging solution for applications that demand light weight and high strength to optimize sustainability, performance and design freedom. Widespread adoption of thermoplastic composites depends on three enablers: new material technologies, efficient large-scale production processes and an accurate, scientific prediction of application performance. SABIC is investing heavily in all three areas,[20]

according to Gino Francato, global business leader of SABIC. Major growth drivers for composites are **increasing demand** for **lightweight materials** in the aerospace & defense, automotive, and wind industry; **corrosion and chemical resistance** requirement in the construction, marine, and pipe & tank industry; **electrical resistivity and high flame retardancy requirement** in the electrical and electronics industry (Figure 7.6). Gino Francato further states.

Figure 7.6 Composites Innovations in Various Applications. (a) Carbon Composite Wheel; (b) Aircraft Winglet.

Customers have told us that they face three hurdles to the introduction of thermoplastic composites in their applications: cost, cycle time and design predictability. Through materials innovation, disruptive automated digital manufacturing and sophisticated predictive engineering capabilities, SABIC intends to remove these hurdles and pave the way for broad adoption of advanced thermoplastic composites across industries and geographies.[20]

Emerging Innovations in Agrochemicals

Innovations in agrochemicals are a rapidly growing area and are changing the conventional way of doing agriculture. These innovation opportunities are broadly categorized as below (Figure 7.7).

It is noteworthy that innovations in **nano-pesticides hold tremendous potential** as they offer a **breakthrough solution over traditional pesticides**; nano-pesticides address both issues by increasing yields and eliminating the negative side effects of conventional pesticides. Over the years we have seen that pesticides and other agrochemicals find their way into our ecosystems, thus contaminating soils, sediments, and waterways, and adversely impacting wildlife. But the emergence of new types of nano-pesticides offers hope for a more environmentally friendly approach. Stacey Harper, scientist at Oregon State University, says, "It won't be long before manufacturers move beyond simply shrinking pesticides into nano-formulations. I expect to see multifunctional nano-pesticides, for example, products equipped with biosensors able to detect pests before releasing the active ingredient within the next 10 years."[21]

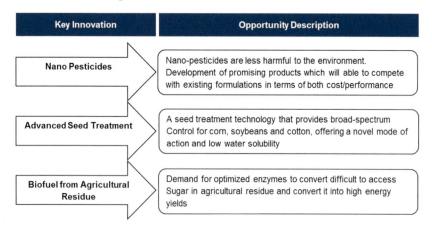

Figure 7.7 Key Innovation Areas for the Agriculture Market.
Source: Lucintel.

Demand for seed treatment[22] is also growing remarkably in agriculture practices as it helps to **prevent seed and soil-borne infections and disease.** In addition, it reduces **germination time, enhances overall productivity,** and **improves crop yield.** Rick Horbury, Customer Advisory Manager of Bayer Crop Science, said, "there has been a swing into seed treatments, with unprecedented demand last year. It got close to being the biggest year ever for seed treatments and it will be bigger this year."[23] Proliferation of sustainable agricultural practices has driven the adoption of biological seed treatment among farmers, especially within government-controlled farming communities. Industry players are making significant investments in R&D to meet the growing demand (Figure 7.8).

Another area identified to be holding good opportunity in the future agriculture market is **biofuel from agricultural residue. Biodegradable, renewable fuels** (biodiesel, bioethanol) represent a **promising alternative energy source** with minimal pollutants like sulfur, nitrous oxides, and carbon dioxide. Markus Rarbach, head of biofuels and derivatives, Clariant, is confident that biofuels and bio-chemicals made from agricultural residue could play a key role in leading today's economy into a more sustainable future by significantly reducing the environmental impacts. As the energy required for the entire process is generated from the residue instead of fossil-based sources, the technology could reduce greenhouse gas emissions by about 95% compared with fossil fuels. The company is currently looking for third parties to license the technology, which could be applied in a wide range of areas including biofuel-powered vehicles and consumer products.[24]

Figure 7.8 **Innovations in Advanced Seed Treatment.**

Revenue Impact and Resulting Growth Opportunity

Our analysis suggests that the agrochemical segment provides the highest growth rate and biggest opportunity. It offers an incredible opportunity to develop new bio- and nano-based products/technologies. This is a key area in which chemical and technology businesses can invest in research and development. **Coatings and polymers** also offer significant innovation opportunities in terms of growth. In coatings, **self-healing** and **temperature management** coating technology are promising, though they are currently at a low level of maturity.

Growth in most opportunities in the chemical industry saw a slowdown in 2020 due to the impact of COVID. Interviews with major manufacturers, such as BASF, LyondellBasell, and Dow Chemical Companies, suggested a decline of 5%–15% in the overall chemical demand in 2020 as compared to 2019. Demand for chemicals is expected to recover gradually as the end-use markets recover. With stay home orders and other health issues, major companies have halted their production or repurposed for production of critical chemicals in the fight against COVID-19. Companies are working to maximize efficiencies, managing inventories to reduce working capital, deferring planned maintenance to save cash, and increasing liquidity. There is less focus on M&A or repurchases, as companies are taking a long view of the recovery, and preparing to sustain as long as possible.

Table 7.1 shows the market size and growth rate for key innovation opportunity areas.

Companies in the chemical industry are focusing on a number of innovation areas. The level of technological maturity is low to moderate in most cases, with significant opportunity for development. Key enablers driving the use of new technologies can be categorized into four main areas:

Table 7.1 Market Opportunities of Various Innovations in the Chemical Industry

Area of Innovation	Current Market Size (2019) (in $ Billion)	CAGR Year (2019–2035) (%)	Market Opportunity
Recyclable paper coating	0.6	9.8	• Packaging
Functional coating for temperature management	1.1	6	• Automotive • Construction

Self-healing powder coatings	0.3	24.5	• Automotive • Electronics
Nanostructured coatings	6.3	23.3	• Automotive • Construction • Industrial
Bioresin in UV coating	0.1	8.4	• Construction • Automotive • Industrial
Green coatings	85.7	4.4	• Construction • Automotive • Industrial
Light cure adhesive technology	1.1	8.6	• Medical • Electronic
Advancements in structural adhesives	13.5	5.4	• Automotive • Construction • Wind energy • Aerospace
Improved nano-fillers	1.0	9.2	• Automotive • Construction equipment
Biodegradable packaging	90	4.6	• Food packaging • Personal/homecare • Pharmaceutical
Biodegradable polymers	5.6	19.4	• Pharmaceutical • Agriculture • Packaging
Bio-based plasticizers	1.5	10.1	• Automotive • Packaging • Consumer goods
Advancements in compounds	67	5.2	• Automotive • Construction • E&E (Electrical and Electronics) • Packaging
Innovation in composite materials	33.4	3	• Transportation • Marine • Wind energy • Aerospace • Pipe & tank • Construction • E&E • Consumer goods
Nano-pesticides	0.7	14	• Agriculture
Advanced seed treatment	4.9	11.2	• Agriculture
Biofuel	136	5.5	• Transportation • Industrial • Others

Source: Lucintel

1. Reduction in emissions from traditional manufacturing currently using fossil fuels
2. Utilization of bio-based sources to manufacture downstream products
3. Utilization of secondary sources such as recyclable materials
4. Development of chemicals based on nanotechnology and nano-materials such as nano-fillers, nano-coatings, and nano-agrochemicals that can improve product performance, reduce cost, and drive innovation at higher levels

Agrochemicals offer significant innovation opportunities; these are in the early stages of the innovation curve. Innovations in polymers and coatings provide greater scope for commercialization success due to lower regulation and relatively high degree of current technological maturity.

Specifically, here's an overview of level of current technology maturity and market potential for key innovation areas in coatings, polymers, and agrochemicals (Figures 7.9–7.12).

Disruptive technologies can change the game for businesses by creating entirely new products and services. Innovations in agrochemicals offer a medium to high degree of disruption, primarily due to developments in nano-pesticides, advanced seed treatment, and biofuel using agricultural residue. The drivers are increasing environmental concerns, stringent government rules, excess use of mineral-based fertilizers and unsafe pesticides coupled with a growing population. Companies taking

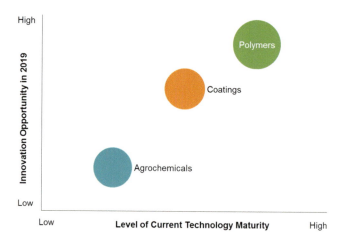

Figure 7.9 Level of Technology Maturity by Innovation Category in the Chemical Industry.
Note: Size of the Bubble Represents Market Size in 2035.
Source: Lucintel.

Chemical 85

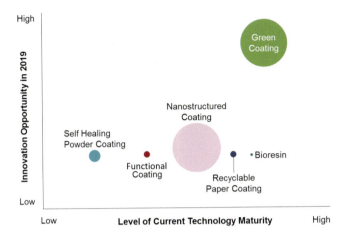

Figure 7.10 Level of Technology Maturity by Innovation Category in the Coatings Market.
Note: Size of the Bubble Represents Market Size in 2035.
Source: Lucintel.

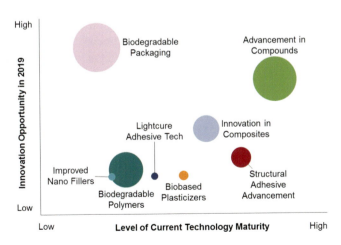

Figure 7.11 Level of Technology Maturity by Innovation Category in the Polymer Market.
Note: Size of the Bubble Represents Market Size in 2035.
Source: Lucintel.

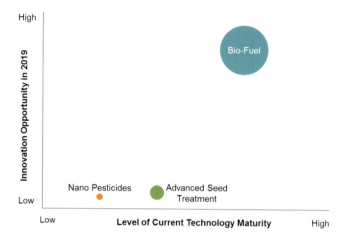

Figure 7.12 Level of Technology Maturity by Innovation Category in the Agrochemicals Market.
Note: Size of the Bubble Represents Market Size in 2035.
Source: Lucintel.

the lead in these areas include BASF, Bayer Crop Science, Monsanto, and Syngenta.

In the polymers and coatings industry, technological maturity is medium. Both industries offer innovation opportunities and greater scope for commercialization success. Regulatory compliance is low in coatings and polymers, but high in the agriculture segment.

Competitive intensity in the agriculture segment is low due to the presence of few players and high growth factors. Coatings and polymers have significant competitive intensity due to the presence of a large number of players.

Highlights

The role of innovation has changed dramatically in recent years in the chemical industry, which is changing the way chemical companies manage their innovation portfolios. Most companies in developed nations are moving away from making of commodity chemicals to more specialized and innovative chemicals as the commodity market is moving to low labor cost countries such as China.

In the area of **sustainable/environment-friendly** innovations, **Arkema, BASF, and DSM** are developing technologies to manufacture bio-based resins. For biodegradable packaging, BASF developed high-quality and versatile bioplastic ecovio®. NatureWorks has developed the Ingeo portfolio of naturally advanced materials made from renewable materials.

The demand for **bio-plasticizers** is growing due to stringent government regulations and rising health concerns of consumers. Consumers/end users are looking for safe, biodegradable, and non-phthalate-based plasticizers for safety and sustainability. **LANXESS** has a global commercial network that sells innovative, phthalate-free plasticizers including ADIMOLL®, MESAMOLL®, ULTRAMOLL®, and UNIMOLL®.

Advancements in **coatings technology** include recyclable paper coatings, functional coatings for temperature management, self-healing coatings, and nano-coatings. The major players have developed products such as **AkzoNobel's EvCote** Water Barrier 3000 coating, **BASF's** coatings technology for passive temperature management, **Solvay's** self-healing coatings enabled by **AMI's technology** with improved performance and a more sustainable solution, **ACTnano's ANG** 100 series of nano-coatings for the protection of electronic devices, and **PPG's** NanoProducts' nanoparticles-based coatings for excellent chip resistance, scratch resistance, and superior sandability for medical devices.

RTP Company has developed laser-markable thermoplastic compounds, including clear substrates that can benefit medical device manufacturers required to comply with the FDA's Unique Device Identification (UDI) program. The compounds have been formulated to allow laser-based high-contrast marks and images, eliminating the need for inks, paints, and dyes. Laser marking on clear resins can be challenging, but RTP is able to compound additives into clear resins that absorb specific wavelengths of energy and create high-contrast marks while the resin remains clear. Laser-markable compounds are available in white, black, or custom colors.

A. Schulman recently launched a series of **Schulamid® PA and Polyfort® PP** compounds[25] for use in automotive applications. The newly developed "RD" (Reduced Density) grades offer a weight-saving potential of up to 26%. Due to the usage of innovative filler systems and intelligent polymer blends, the RD grades fulfill the highest technical requirements. Some of these material solutions can be used directly, without any changes in tool design or in equipment, which represents important savings for the OEM. In addition to the lightweight aspect, a carbon footprint reduction of up to 59% can be achieved by using A. Schulman's RD compounds.

SABIC's proprietary **ULTEM™ resin** and Kringlan's proprietary three-dimensional composite design capabilities can be used to replace traditional materials, such as metal and aluminum alloys, helping reduce weight and emissions, and potentially saving manufacturing costs.

88 Emerging Innovations by Industry

In the fields of adhesives and polymers, examples include **Loctite® INDIGO™ Light Cure Adhesives,** a revolutionary technology that can rely solely on low-energy light in the visible spectrum and **Sika's** Power crash-durable adhesives.

Most of the innovations are a step change in existing product performance. In the area of **agrochemicals,** companies such as **Syngenta, BASF, DuPont,** and **Dow Agrosciences** are developing disruptive products with nano-agrochemical capabilities to increase crop activity and yield without a harmful impact on the environment.

Horizon Planning Implications

To put these research findings in context, the chart below categorizes each opportunity area in terms of the Expanded Horizons Model[26] described in Chapter 1.

Definition of Each Innovation Type: Horizon 1 = Incremental, line extension, continuous improvement; **Horizon 2** = New to company or new to a sector; **Horizon 3** = Disruptive, new to the world (Table 7.2).

Most of the opportunities can be categorized as Horizons 1 and 2 depending on strategy and investment. Trends and indicators would suggest the following approaches for those investing in chemical development:

Table 7.2 Horizon Planning Implications for the Chemical Industry

Area of Innovation	Horizon 1	Horizon 2	Horizon 3
Chemicals			
Recyclable paper coating	Y	Y	Y
Functional coating for temperature management	Y	Y	
Self-healing powder coatings	Y	Y	Y
Nano-coatings for medical devices & electronic applications	Y	Y	
Bioresin in UV coating	Y	Y	
Green coating for multiple features	Y	Y	
Light cure adhesive technology	Y	Y	Y
Structural adhesives	Y	Y	
Improved nano-fillers	Y	Y	Y
Biodegradable packaging	Y	Y	
Biodegradable polymers	Y	Y	
Bio-based plasticizers	Y	Y	
Compounds	Y	Y	
Composites	Y	Y	Y
Nano-pesticides	Y	Y	Y
Advanced seed treatment	Y	Y	Y
Biofuel from agricultural residue	Y	Y	Y

Source: **Innovation**edge, LLC.
Content Source: Lucintel

- **Recyclable Paper Coating:** With its high disruptive potential and projected growth rate, Horizon 2 and 3 opportunities are great. In particular, advances in recyclability and excellent barrier properties have the potential for breakthrough products with customizable and environmental benefits. **Horizons 2 and 3 suggested.**
- **Functional Coating for Temperature Management:** This innovation is suitable for energy-efficient and/or environment-friendly products. **Horizons 1 and/or 2 are most likely,** though identifying untapped customer needs could lead to Horizon 3 endeavors.
- **Self-Healing Powder Coatings:** With its high disruptive potential and projected growth rate, **Horizons 2 and 3** opportunities are great.
- **Nano-coatings for Medical Device & Electronic Applications:** The innovation in this category can be a launchpad for game-changing devices by preventing the transmission of infectious diseases from contact with medical devices or other surfaces. **Horizons 1 and/or 2 are suitable,** though identifying untapped customer needs could lead to Horizon 3 endeavors.
- **Bioresin in UV Coating:** Within this category, promising solutions such as reduction in energy consumption, pollution, and VOC emissions can be created utilizing eco-friendly products. **Horizons 1 and/or 2 suggested.**
- **Green Coating:** With multiple features, it has the largest current opportunity as well as technological maturity, making it suitable as a core or incremental activity. Green coating demand is driven primarily by increasing consumer interest in buying environmentally friendly products and the growing popularity of green building standards. **Horizons 1 and/or 2 are suitable.**
- **Light Cure Adhesive Technology:** Within this category, promising solutions such as reduction in energy consumption, fast curing, and low VOC emissions can result in more eco-friendly products that have better performance. **Horizons 1, 2, or 3 suggested.**
- **Advancements in Structural Adhesives:** Structural adhesives offer multiple features such as bonding dissimilar substrates with high structural stability. Structural adhesives have the largest current opportunity as well as technological maturity. **Horizons 1, 2, or 3 suggested.**
- **Improved Nano-Fillers:** In particular, advances in nano-fillers offer both excellent potential and projected growth rate. **Horizons 1 and/or 2 suggested.**
- **Biodegradable Polymer and Packaging[27]:** These products offer great potential with high growth rate; the largest market opportunity is in the bio-polymers market. **Horizons 1 and/or 2 suggested.**
- **Bio-Based Plasticizers:** They offer disruptive potential. Horizon 2 and 3 opportunities are great. Bio-based plasticizers can capitalize on the growing trend in the consumer market. **Horizons 1, 2, or 3 suggested.**

- **Advancements in Compounds:** Compounds are the largest current opportunity with high technological maturity, making them suitable for a core or incremental activity. **Horizons 1 and/or 2 are suitable.**
- **Composites: They** offer disruptive opportunity as well as technological maturity, making them suitable for incremental activity. In particular, composites have become the best alternative to traditional materials, such as steel, aluminum, and wood, and have gained popularity among OEMs and fabricators for superior performance. **Horizons 1 and/or 2 are suitable based on application.**
- **Nano-Pesticides:** With its high disruptive potential and projected growth rate, Horizon 1 and 2 opportunities are great. In particular, nano-based pesticides are promising in this respect as they address both issues such as higher yields and negative side effects of conventional pesticides. **Horizons 1 and/or 2 are suitable.**
- **Advanced Seed Treatment:** This area offers moderate potential and projected growth rate, Horizon 1 and 2 opportunities are great. Demand for seed treatment is growing in agriculture practices as it helps prevent seed- and soil-borne infections and diseases. **Horizons 1 and/or 2 are suitable.**
- **Biofuel from Agricultural Residue:** With its high disruptive potential and moderate projected growth rate, biofuels and bio-chemicals made from agricultural residues could play a key role in leading today's economy into a more sustainable future by significantly reducing the environmental impacts. **Horizons 1 and/or 2 suitable.**

Our study concludes that, overall, all the innovation areas in the chemical industry hold good growth potential with expansion in the overall industry. Formulating strategies according to the megatrends will make companies ripe for innovation both in the short term and in the long term.

References

1. "CEO statement", *AkzoNobel*, 2017.
2. Lucintel publication, Growth Opportunities in the Global Green Coatings Market, 2016.
3. Lucintel publication, Opportunities in the Biodegradable Mulch Film Market: Market size, Trends and Growth Analysis, 2021.
4. "New biodegradable barrier coating for paper and cardboard packaging", *Bioplastics*, Nov. 14, 2017.
5. "Energy saving trust", *Dulux Trade Paint*, Jan. 8, 2018.
6. Jenny Eagle, "Dow Paper Coatings sees a shift towards compostable and biodegradable paper products", Bakery and Snacks, Jun. 27, 2015.
7. Lucintel publication, Self-Healing Material Market 2019-2024: Trends, Forecast, and Opportunity Analysis, 2021.
8. Jane Benson, "Natick investigates self-healing protective clothing", *U.S. Army*, Nov. 30, 2015.

Chemical 91

9. "Dragonfly-Inspired Nano Coating Kills Bacteria Upon Contact", *A*STAR*, Mar. 28, 2018.
10. Lucintel publication, Global UV Curable Resin Market Report: Trends, Forecast and Competitive Analysis, 2015.
11. "Soy resin used in variety of products", *United Soybean Board*, Mar. 03, 2016.
12. Lucintel publication, Opportunities and Competitive Analysis of the Global Waterborne Coatings Market, 2017.
13. Kerry Pianoforte, "'Green' coatings market is growing", *Coatings World*, Mar. 29, 2010.
14. Lucintel publication, Technology Trends in the Global Structural Adhesive Market, 2021.
15. John Huetter, "Experts: Structural adhesives cheaper, lighter, faster than other joining methods for OEMs", *Repairer Driven News*, Mar. 19, 2016.
16. "ecovio® – Biobased and compostable polymer", BASF.
17. Jessie Waldheim, "US PolyOne promotes bio-plasticizers to replace phthalates", *ICIS*, Mar. 24, 2015.
18. Lucintel publication, Bio-Plasticizer Market Report: Trends, Forecast and Competitive Analysis, 2021.
19. Lucintel publication, Trends, Opportunities and Competitive Analysis of the Global Composites Market, 2021.
20. Stephen Moore, "SABIC showcases disruptive innovation in thermoplastic composite materials at JEC World 2018", *Plastics Today*, Mar. 07, 2018.
21. Virginia Gewin, "Everything you need to know about nanopesticides", *The Fern*, Jan. 21, 2015.
22. Lucintel publication, Growth Opportunities in the Global Genetically Modified Seed Market, 2017.
23. "Seed treatment used for crop protection", *Farm Weekly*, Mar. 29, 2017.
24. Thijs Bouwens, "Clariant's sunliquid® cellulosic ethanol technology to support china's 2020 bioethanol-gasoline mandate", *Clariant*, Nov. 06, 2017.
25. Lucintel publication, Opportunities and Competitive Analysis of the Polypropylene Compound Market, 2021.
26. **Innovation**edge, LLC., Expanded Horizons Model ©
27. Lucintel publication, Strategic Technology Trends in the Global Biodegradable Plastics Market, 2021.

Chapter 8

Building Construction

In this chapter, we consider the following aspects of the construction industry:

– Emerging Innovations
– Revenue Impact and Resulting Growth Opportunities
– Horizon Planning Implications

Emerging Innovations

The construction industry is ranked among the world's oldest, largest, and most diverse industries in terms of employment and value of output. Its technologies are relatively mature. However, rapid development in automation technology, information technology, and pre-fabrication has led to the introduction of computer-integrated construction systems and efficient housing and commercial buildings. With the emergence of new materials and advanced technologies, the industry is focusing on light-weight and green material contents. To achieve greater efficiencies, better accuracy rates, reduced manpower, and faster production time, many are turning to robotics and 3D printing for making parts and structures. Mike Pavic, Fastbrick, CEO said,

> When you look at the way things are happening, it's hard to conceive that 20 or 30 years from now we will still see men carrying bricks to a bricklayer, shovelling sand cement into a mixer and then pouring it into a wheelbarrow and wheeling it over planks and drums. We believe young people will see robotic construction as a good career choice in the future.[1]

Because the market is so diverse, tremendous innovation opportunities exist for different applications. In particular, green buildings, innovative materials, and automated technologies are ripe for growth.

DOI: 10.4324/9781003177906-12

Building Construction

Our analysis suggests that, in the next ten years, manufacturers will increasingly move toward smart and intelligent buildings. Some examples of smart buildings are NASA Sustainability Base in Moffett Field, California, by William McDonough Partners; the Duke Energy Center, Charlotte, North Carolina; Mansion ZCB, Hong Kong, by Ronald Lu & Partners, Bahrain World Trade Centre by Atkins; Pacific Controls Building, Dubai, by Aedas Architects. Artificial intelligence (AI) in building information modeling (BIM) will bring a paradigm shift to the construction industry. Applying AI will lead to reduced prices, better safety, and more accurate and rapid assembly, commented Tim Chapman, Director of Arup. These smart, intelligent buildings are the epitome of innovation in today's environment. They possess complex information networks operated by computer technologies – often going beyond automated lighting, shading, and HVAC configurations. They feature advanced, real-time controls of the building's energy efficiency, comfort levels, accessibility, fire alarm systems, and other elements.

An example is NASA's Sustainability Base in Moffett Field, California, completed by William McDonough Partners. The intelligent building is crescent-shaped and boasts an intelligent control technology inspired by the agency's Aviation Safety Program. This technology is used to control different zones within the building and provide real-time data about airflow through the entire structure. William McDonough Partners is known for its cradle-to-cradle design approach and use of renewable, recyclable, or recycled materials.

By 2030, we expect most buildings to be more efficient, green, and smart in comparison to today's buildings. Companies are setting future targets and have begun working to achieve them (Figure 8.1).

Figure 8.1 Intelligent Buildings.

For better understanding, we have provided a broad categorization of the top innovation opportunities in the construction market as below (Figure 8.2).

Our research identifies **green buildings** to be holding one of the most extraordinary growth opportunities. Over the last few years in the construction industry, the green building movement has drawn everyone's attention and thus gained momentum globally. New technologies and new materials are constantly being developed to complement the practices in creating greener structures (Figure 8.3).

Another area showing continuous advancements is wireless and automated technologies for homes and will be increasing in the future. **Smart homes** offer a huge investment opportunity in the global construction industry. During our study we found that the construction industry is

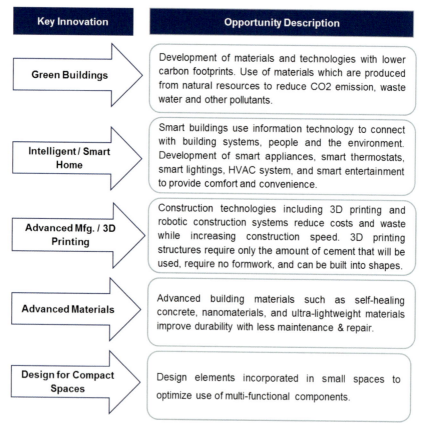

Figure 8.2 Key Areas of Opportunities in Innovation for the Construction Industry.
Source: Lucintel.

Figure 8.3 Innovations in Green Building.

one of the least automated industries and **advanced manufacturing technologies** such as robotics and 3D printing can bring significant benefits to the industry as well as to the environment. These advanced technologies hold the highest growth potential in the near future. Companies including Contour Crafting Corporation, CyBe Construction, and Apis Cor have already created, tested, and used 3D printers for construction purposes. Similarly, there are several types of robots that are poised to break into the construction market. There are 3D printing robots that can build large buildings on demand; also, there are construction robots for brick laying and masonry, and even robots that lay an entire street at one time (Figure 8.4).

Components with reduced weight, high performance, high strength, and cost compatibility will be widely accepted by builders to meet global emission reduction and efficiency improvement goals worldwide. New efficient materials hold huge potential for innovation in this industry. The emergence of **fiber-reinforced composite material with polymeric, metallic, or ceramic matrix** properties presents innovation opportunities for manufacturers to go beyond classic lightweight materials such as high-strength steel, aluminum, concrete, and ceramics. **Lightweight concrete** with self-healing properties has already gained the attention of consumers and is being accepted widely (Figure 8.5).

As per United Nations (UN) estimates, 68% of the world's population will live in urban areas by mid-century as compared to 55% today, due to overall population growth and migration from rural areas.[2] This growth is creating demand for sustainable cities which are **compact** and **connected** and designed to preserve more open space and make more

96 Emerging Innovations by Industry

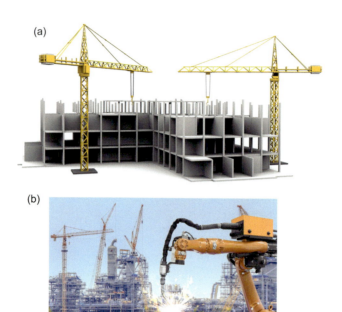

Figure 8.4 Different Types of Advanced Manufacturing Techniques in the Construction Industry. (a) 3D Printed Structure; (b) Robots in Construction.

Figure 8.5 Innovations in Advanced Materials for the Construction Industry. (a) Graphene; (b) GFRP.

efficient use of land and resources. **Micro apartments/tiny homes** are thus gaining popularity (Figure 8.6).

To support the concept of compact spaces, companies have come up with different design solutions and innovations; for example, Duravit

Building Construction

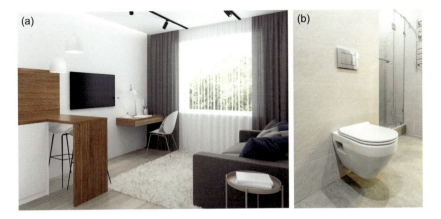

Figure 8.6 Innovations Accompanying the Idea of Compact Designing. (a) Compact Room Design; (b) Wall-Hung Dual-Flush Toilet.

launched the first **foldable shower,** which is a shower enclosure that can be folded after use to save space. TOTO developed a micro-toilet design for bathrooms as small as 9 square feet (0.84 meters). The **Aquia Wall-Hung Dual Flush toilet** is mounted onto the wall – hiding its water tank out of sight and saving space in small bathrooms. Washing clothes in a tiny house requires a small-sized washing machine. Traditional washing machines are 27 inches wide and about 30 inches deep. **Hand-operated washing machines, like Wonderwash,** are also available for tiny houses. The Wonderwash unit weighs just 6 pounds and its dimensions are 12 inches × 12 inches × 16 inches.

Revenue Impact and Growth Opportunities

Our analysis suggests that in the construction industry, **green buildings** provide the largest opportunity over the forecast period. **Smart homes** and **designs for compact spaces** offer incredible opportunities to develop new technology and where R&D investment by manufacturers is recommended. Manufacturers can realize significant opportunities in advanced manufacturing/3D printing, advanced material solutions, design for compact spaces, smart homes, and green buildings.

The COVID-19 pandemic affected the growth of the construction industry in 2020. The current global shutdown has halted many construction projects globally, mainly affecting the mid-level subcontractors. The market will recover in 2021 and beyond.

Table 8.1 shows the market size and growth rate for key innovation opportunity areas:

98 Emerging Innovations by Industry

Table 8.1 Innovation Opportunities in the Construction Industry

Area of Innovation	Current Market Size (2019) (in $ Billion)	CAGR (2019– 2035) (%)	Market Opportunity
Green buildings	217	9.8	• Energy-efficient insulation • Recyclable resources and solar power • Water percolation/water harvesting • Composting toilets
Intelligent/smart buildings	74	7.6	• Smart meters • Connected appliances • Energy-efficient HVAC system • Connected thermostats, smart lighting • Connected door locks, video surveillance • Fire sprinklers and extinguishers • Intruder alarms
Advanced manu-facturing/3D printing	0.7	17	• 3D printing for house construction • Construction robots • 5D BIM (building information modeling) • Drone • Solar roads
Advanced material solutions	8	5	• Super-material graphene • Self-healing concrete • Lightweight materials (CFRP, GFRP) • 3D printed bricks • Nano-materials • High-performance glass • High-performance mortars and concretes • Composites
Design for compact space	36	8.7	• Tiny apartments • Hand-powered washing machines • Tiny house furniture (day beds, Murphy beds, loft and bunk beds, cots or folding beds) • Pre-fab kitchens • Tiny appliances • Shower inserts/wet baths

Source: Lucintel

We found the construction industry to be highly price sensitive, which means technology must be proven and low cost to encourage widespread adoption. Innovations in advanced manufacturing/3D printing and design for compact spaces offer a high degree of disruption. Large-scale **3D printers** capable of 3D printing metal and concrete are being adapted to print large structures and realize complex projects. Construction of **micro apartments/tiny apartment/tiny homes** is increasing in Hong Kong, New York, Japan, and other mega-cities due to the shortage of urban space. Development of **robotics** furniture, tiny kitchens, micro washing machines, and compact appliances and furniture is supporting lifestyle ease in tiny homes. **Green construction, smart building, and advanced material** solutions are relatively mature innovation areas as compared to 3D printing and design for compact spaces.

> We wanted to make spaces in homes, offices and hotels much more functional and efficient but also more intelligent by bringing robotics into play. When you have so many people moving into the same place, you need to start being more efficient about how you use the spaces,[3]

as said by Hasier Larrea, Founder and CEO, Ori.

In terms of technological maturity, advanced manufacturing/3D printing requires significant investment to develop commercial readiness. The speed of introduction of these new technologies depends not only on technical feasibility, but on quality and cost of the product.

The chart below provides an overview of the level of current technology maturity and market potential for key innovation areas in the construction industry (Figure 8.7).

We found that innovations in **green buildings, smart homes,** and **advanced materials** offer enormous opportunities at varied levels of technology maturity. **Advanced manufacturing/3D printing** and **design for compact spaces** provide a smaller opportunity currently and require significant technology maturity and development for commercialization success.

While new technologies are proliferating, the construction industry is very slow in embracing them. First, companies tend to have tight budget constraints and may not have the funds available to purchase and implement a new technology or solution. Further, implementation may require hiring more staff and training employees to use the new technology effectively. These additional costs are prohibitive in many cases. Moreover, the risk associated with adopting new technologies can be high. Large firms require significant investments to integrate new technologies into their practices, and the adoption process can severely affect normal operations. Firms seeking a competitive edge cannot simply adopt new

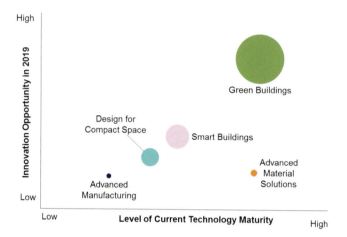

Figure 8.7 Level of Technology Maturity by Innovation Category in the Construction Industry.
Note: Size of the Bubble Represents Market Size in 2035.
Source: Lucintel.

technologies; they must integrate them efficiently and optimize their usage to see return on investment. However, as the cost of acquisition goes down and the need for differentiation increases, the rate and pace of new technology adoption will increase rapidly. Nonetheless, green buildings are being developed now, and smart cities are being planned. Companies are experimenting with 3D printing and other automated technologies.

Highlights

Green Buildings: Jerry Yudelson, President of the Green Building Initiative, said:

> We know that buildings are responsible for more than 40% of US carbon emissions and more than 30% of total global emissions. Promoting green building and sustainable operations are essential steps in reducing and eventually eliminating carbon emissions that contribute directly to global climate change.[4]

Many companies such as **Tarkett, Johns Manville, Owens Corning, Huntsman, J & J Flooring, Roca,** and **Alphi** are developing green technologies with recycled material or are developing products which are energy efficient. **Tarkett** developed narrative flooring with 90% recycled content. **Johns Manville's** flexible duct insulation is formaldehyde-free and manufactured using bio-based binders. **Huntsman, Owens Corning, and Collodin** jointly developed TICO PUR energy-efficient windows and doors. **J & J Flooring** developed hybrid flooring, which has 50% less environmental impact and contains 50% recycled content.

Smart Homes[5, 6, 7]: Laurie Aaron, Executive Vice President at Wave-Lynx Technologies Corporation, is confident that there is continuous innovation in the access control market; the introduction of completely contactless entry is on the way but it will take 15–20 years to reach the goal. I do see that coming but we are years away since this industry moves at a very slow pace in terms of innovation, but I think the time is ripe for disruption. We have partners that are cloud-based access control systems and they absolutely have that vision of contactless entry; the cloud talking to the device and the device back to the cloud into the hardware that unlocks the door.[8] **ADT, Robert Bosch, Vivint,** and **Honeywell** are developing technologies to manufacture connected devices. ADT launched the ADT Pulse app. Through this app, subscribers turn on lights, monitor carbon monoxide, arm alarms, and even control heating with their voice. **Honeywell** launched Tuxedo Touch, the touchscreen security and home automation controller that can serve as the central hub of a connected home or business.

Advanced Building Materials[9, 10, 11]: **Knauf, Kone, USG, GAF, DOW, RAK Ceramics, BASF, Saint Gobain,** and **Tarkett** are developing products with better performance through advanced materials. Knauf launched Plasterboard that eliminates the requirement of air conditioners and reduces energy consumption. Kone launched Ultrarope, a lightweight and high-strength rope made with carbon fiber. GAF launched a triple-laminate shingle which is fire resistant, algae resistant, and more durable. Dow's XENERGY roofing insulation provides 11% improved insulation due to infra-red blocking particles which scatter and reflect heat radiation within the foamboard. RAK Ceramics developed extra-large sized slabs, which are twice as strong as traditional porcelain.

Other major areas of innovation are 3D printing and design for compact spaces. **Duravit, TOTO, Resource Furniture, Wanderwash, Yirego, and Sanwa** are some of the leading players operating in design for compact spaces.

Horizon Planning Implications

To put these research findings in context, the chart below categorizes each opportunity area in terms of the Expanded Horizons Model[12] described in Chapter 1.

Definition of each Innovation Type: Horizon 1 = Incremental, line extension, continuous improvement; **Horizon 2** = New to company or new to a sector; **Horizon 3** = Disruptive, new to the world (Table 8.2).

102 Emerging Innovations by Industry

Table 8.2 Horizon Planning Implications for the Construction Industry

Area of Innovation	Horizon 1	Horizon 2	Horizon 3
Green building	Y	Y	
Intelligent/smart home	Y	Y	Y
Advanced manufacturing/3D printing	Y	Y	Y
Advanced building material solutions	Y	Y	
Design for compact spaces	Y	Y	Y

Source: **Innovation**edge, LLC.
Content Source: Lucintel

Most of the innovations can be categorized as Horizons 1 and 2. Trends and indicators would suggest the following approach for those investing in the construction industry:

- **Green Building:** This area has the largest current opportunity. With its high potential and projected growth rate, Horizons 1 and 2 opportunities are great. In particular, advances in energy-saving technology can lead to development of breakthrough products with significant cost-saving benefits. **Horizons 1 and/or 2 suggested.**
- **Intelligent/Smart Home**[13, 14, 15, 16]**:** This category can be a launch-pad for game-changing smart devices that give homeowners more connection and control. Smart lighting and smart appliances can make a home more convenient and comfortable. This innovation area has a huge investment potential and a strong growth forecast. **Horizons 1 and 2 suggested** although identifying untapped customer needs could lead to **Horizon 3** endeavors.
- **Advanced Manufacturing/3D Printing**[17]**:** This area has the highest growth forecast along with low technological maturity, making it suitable as a core or incremental activity; 3D printing, robotics, augmented and virtual reality (AR&VR) could provide the most disruptive innovations for the construction industry. **Horizon 1, 2, or 3 suitable.**
- **Advanced Building Material Solutions:** Within this category, promising technologies such as lightweight materials, self-healing concrete, and high-performance glass, mortars, insulation, etc., can be developed. **Horizon 1 and/or 2 suggested.**
- **Design for Compact Spaces:** This area has a good investment potential and growth forecast with low technological maturity. Transformable furniture, tiny toilets, and pre-fab trailers, kitchens, and interior objects can be innovated. **Horizon 1, 2 or 3 suggested.**

The five key opportunity areas in the construction industry all have high growth potential as the overall industry continues to expand. The megatrend of population and urbanization, combined with accelerated technology development, makes this industry ripe for innovation, both short and long term.

References

1. Adele Peters, "This bricklaying robot can build low-cost houses in two days", *Fast Company*, Nov. 08, 2016.
2. "68% of the world population projected to live in urban areas by 2050, says UN", *United Nations*, May 16, 2018.
3. Kate Rogers, "Robotic furniture to hit the market for tiny apartments", *CNBC*, Sep. 19, 2016.
4. "UN climate change report strengthens case for green building", *Green Building Initiative*, Nov. 05, 2014.
5. Lucintel publication, Growth Opportunities in the Global Smart Home Market, 2020.
6. Lucintel publication, Opportunities in the Smart Appliances Market: Market size, Trends and Growth Analysis, 2021.
7. Lucintel publication, Top Technology Trends that will Impact Global Smart Meter Market Landscape, 2021.
8. Steve Lasky, "Disruption and innovation are separated by a fine line", *Security Infowatch*, Nov. 10, 2017.
9. Lucintel publication, Emerging Technology Trends in the Global Graphene Market, 2021.
10. Lucintel publication, Opportunities and Competitive Analysis of the Glass Fiber Reinforced Plastic Market, 2021.
11. Lucintel publication, Trends, Opportunities and Competitive Analysis of the Carbon Fiber Reinforced Plastic (CFRP) Market, 2020.
12. **Innovation**edge, LLC., Expanded Horizons Model ©
13. Lucintel publication, Smart Thermostats Market Report: Trends, Forecast and Competitive Analysis, 2021.
14. Lucintel publication, Trends, Opportunities and Competitive Analysis of the Global Smart Lighting Market, 2017.
15. Lucintel publication, Growth Opportunities in the Global Video Surveillance Market, 2020.
16. Lucintel publication, Top Technology Trends Reshaping Global Intruder Alarm Market, 2021.
17. Lucintel publication, Opportunities in the 3D Concrete Printing Market: Growth Trends, Forecast and Competitive Analysis, 2021.

Chapter 9

Electronics

In this chapter, we consider the following aspects of the electronics industry:

– Emerging Innovations
– Revenue Impact and Resulting Growth Opportunities
– Horizon Planning Implications

Emerging Innovations

The global electronics industry is one of the largest and fastest-growing manufacturing sectors in the world. In our study, we found that the demand for electronic products continues to rise, driven by such factors as the growing use of electronic devices in daily life, shorter product life cycles, and technological advancements. Sensors, cloud computing, big data, and flexible electronics are creating new markets and applications as well as a demand for new equipment/products.

We have presented a broad categorization of the top innovation opportunities in the electronics industry in Figure 9.1.

Organic light emitting diodes (OLEDs)[1] are creating new market opportunities for display and electronic device manufacturers. Superior viewing experiences and entertainment quality, better diagnostics, and smarter driver assistance systems are enabled by two promising technologies known as the OLED technology and the quantum dot light emitting diode (QLED) technology. **Technologically advanced products such as OLED and QLED are anticipated to boost the advanced display market.** Brian Kwon, Executive Vice President and CEO of the LG Home Entertainment Company, said that LG focused on gaining business momentum and positioning itself for the future by actively promoting the OLED TV line-up. "We intend to significantly expand the market penetration of LG OLED TVs which have been receiving superb reviews as the next-generation TV. Collectively, our OLED technologies

DOI: 10.4324/9781003177906-13

Electronics 105

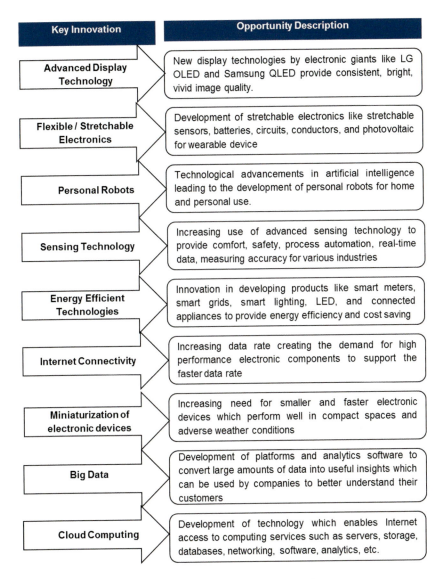

Figure 9.1 Key Innovation Areas in the Electronics Industry.
Source: Lucintel.

will propel us forward as a trusted leader in the global premium TV market"[2] (Figure 9.2).

A new era of electronics is emerging, enabled by flexible hybrid electronics (FHE). Flexible displays have been with us for a while, but new products are appearing that will let us wear our smartphones

Figure 9.2 Innovations in OLED TV.

on our wrist. Flexible displays are driving a great deal of innovation. Human-skin-like materials are incorporating a host of sensors. All are driving demands for innovation in FHE,[3] as said by Dr. Melissa Grupen-Shemansky, CTO of SEMI FlexTech. **Advances in flexible and stretchable electronics can bring significant benefits to medical patients as well as electronic device users.** Stretchable circuits[4] were first developed by using wavy interconnectors that could stretch. Researchers also found ways to stretch silicon. The initial products in the market were body-worn sensors to track health-related data. Technological innovations continue to take place including biodegradable implants and stretchable sensors, which can be used in the development of artificial skin.

We find significant innovations in the use of robots for various applications. During the COVID-19 period in 2020, we saw an increased use of robots in hospitals and factories. For example, a robot can allow healthcare workers to remotely take temperatures and measure blood pressure and oxygen saturation from patients hooked up to a ventilator. Robots[5] can also disinfect hospitals, airports, factories, workspaces, and sensitive areas with ultraviolet light. Drones and robots are also used to watch for public works and public safety to identify violations of stay-at-home restrictions, etc. Similarly, **personal robots have the potential to**

transform our lives. The latest technological advancements have resulted in the introduction of humanoid robots which can assist in household chores as well as in commercial settings. In the future, personal robots are also expected to provide medical assistance and be deployed in business settings (Figure 9.3).

Advancement in sensor technology[6] is creating new market opportunities in industries including robotics, automotive, aerospace, medical devices, and civil infrastructure. Sensors play a crucial role in data tracking and analysis; they are used to record variations and send information to the processor for next steps. The ability to sense variations is regarded as one of the most important inventions as sensors are often used in devices which improve quality of life. Sensors support a variety of applications, including navigation, security, measuring health-related data, and studying the environment. Sensors are increasingly used to gather real-time data on pressure, temperature, moisture, distance, air pollution, and more (Figure 9.4).

The radar[7] (radio detection and ranging) and lidar[8] (light detection and ranging) sensing technologies are used in the navigation systems of vehicles. Both sensing technologies detect obstacles by emitting signals.

As we have seen in the other chapters, energy-efficient technologies are gaining prominence in various industries as they reduce cost and CO_2 emissions. Energy-efficient technologies minimize the carbon footprint and cost-effectively reduce emission of harmful gases into the atmosphere. To deal with climate change, emission of greenhouse gases must be reduced 50% by 2050. Automated meter readers, smart meters, and smart grids are being introduced to monitor energy usage. In the future, software is expected to increase the role of renewable resources in

Figure 9.3 **Innovations in Personal Robot.**

108 Emerging Innovations by Industry

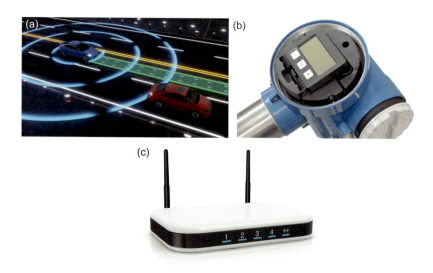

Figure 9.4 Innovations in Sensors. (a) Lidar Sensor; (b) Radar Sensor; (c) Wireless Sensor.

Figure 9.5 Different Types of Energy-Efficient Devices. (a) Smart Lighting; (b) Smart Meter.

smart grids to improve energy infrastructure. Since energy-efficient devices consume less power, they are by nature cost-effective (Figure 9.5).

Internet connectivity is one of the most transformative technologies today as it enables unprecedented levels of information acquisition, information sharing, and social interaction. Internet use has increased as smartphones, smart homes, connected cars, and other connected devices have been introduced and Wi-Fi access has expanded (Figure 9.6).

Another market which is expected to experience high growth will be innovations in the **miniaturization of electronic products.** Today's electronic products are becoming smaller with more embedded functionality.

Electronics 109

Figure 9.6 Internet Connectivity.

Figure 9.7 Miniaturization of Electronic Devices.

Micro-Electro-Mechanical Systems (MEMS)[9] technology has played a major role. Due to their superior performance, they are expected to be widely deployed in IoT devices. Miniaturization also continues to revolutionize circuit design. Pocket calculators and electronic watches are some examples of miniaturization (Figure 9.7).

Big data technology has the potential to transform sectors such as healthcare, insurance, and retail. Big data platforms and analytics software help to convert large amounts of data into useful insights. Cloud data centers eliminate the cost required to set up an on-premise infrastructure. David Gorbet, Vice President of Product Strategy for MarkLogic, explains that the increase in data complexity is the biggest challenge that every IT department and CIO must address. Businesses across industries have to not only store the data but also be able to leverage it quickly and effectively to derive business value. There are many applications where simply being able to comb through large volumes of complex data from multiple sources via interactive queries can give organizations new insights about their products, customers, services, etc. Being able to combine these interactive data explorations with some analytics and visualization can produce new insights that would otherwise be hidden.[10]

The technology can be used to study customer choices and current market trends and to identify hidden correlations. Big data platforms include data warehousing, machine learning, and data processing, along with providing data security and governance (Figure 9.8).

Cloud-based technologies are among the newest innovations in the electronics industry. Cloud technology makes it possible to access any information from anywhere, anytime. It eliminates the need to be at the same place as the hardware holding the stored data and helps reduce the cost of purchasing and keeping memory devices. There are different types of cloud that users can subscribe to, depending on their needs (Figure 9.9).

Cloud computing technology is gaining popularity across a variety of industries for business support. As per our analysis, cloud computing is one of the largest markets and is forecast to grow at double digits during the next five to ten years.

> Every business should engage in its digital transformation and build a cloud solution development plan. The evolution of cloud computing

Figure 9.8 Innovation in Big Data Technology.

Figure 9.9 Innovations in Cloud Computing Technologies.

in the coming year will focus on Hybrid cloud and cloud-based IoT technologies adoption as soon as 5G is ready. As connectivity is the key for digital transformation of our environment, it is true that we are still missing the 5G technologies to allow this IoT revolution. But it is just a question of time and it is better to get ready now,[11]

as commented by Michel Cui, Head of Mid-market & Internet Industry, Alibaba Cloud Europe. The biggest trend in cloud-based technology is **infrastructures as a service** (IaaS) in which all infrastructure components are maintained by cloud providers such as servers, software, storage, and hardware. This eliminates costs associated with data center space, network equipment, software, and servers. Another trend in cloud-based systems is cloud automation, including IT resources and automated processes. Cloud automation allows businesses to select programs they want to use to manage their systems.

Revenue Impact and Resulting Growth Opportunities

Our research suggests that cloud computing and personal robots offer the highest rate of growth during the forecast period. Cloud computing is also found to be the largest opportunity where companies have significantly invested to commercialize the technology. Apart from cloud computing, sensing technology offers a significant opportunity to develop new technology to address emerging market needs. Companies can, with the right strategy, realize significant opportunities in advanced displays, energy-efficiency technology, miniaturization of electronic devices, flexible and stretchable electronics, and internet connectivity.

Short-term growth of the above-mentioned opportunities will be hampered due to the pandemic, but the impact of COVID is mild for the E&E industry when compared to other industries. Interviews with major manufacturers, such as Apple, Foxconn, and Samsung, suggest a decline of ~10% in the overall industry revenue based on decreased demand in 2020 due to COVID-19. E&E-based companies are being significantly affected by supply chain challenges during COVID, because of the industry's reliance on the APAC region for the supply of critical components.

Dr. Joan Vrtis, CTO of Multek, is confident that FPCs are expected to grow at a rapid pace and will have huge potential, mainly due to an increasing trend toward wearables, miniaturization of electronics, and increasing component density per FPC board to enable higher functionality. He said, "we have already started working to tap growing opportunity in the market, designing more effective and efficient technology to meet the need for high frequency response, high speed data transmission & low data loss."[12] We also see good potential for FPC growth in 5G telecommunication network and in the IOTs market, including wearable electronics, smart vehicles, etc. Flexible and stretchable electronics, advanced display, personal robots, big data, and cloud computing offer a high degree of **disruption**. Flexible and stretchable electronics devices offer a novel platform to interface with soft tissues for robotic feedback and control, regenerative medicine, and continuous health monitoring. In the future, such devices for cardiology, dermatology, electrophysiology, and sweat diagnostics applications may replace conventional clinical tools. Robots are already changing the way we live and will become more commonplace for everyday usage.

Table 9.1 shows the market size and growth rate for key innovation opportunity areas.

The electronics industry is known for rapid technology change including the use of new sensors, advanced display technologies, personal robots, and the development of more energy-efficient systems. Household appliance manufacturers are integrating their products with IoT technology to make customers' lives more comfortable and convenient. Many electronic equipment companies are using robotics and automation to improve plant efficiency and productivity. Sensors are being used to improve efficiencies and reduce potential breakdowns.

Figure 9.10 shows the technology readiness in the electronics industry based on the size of the innovation opportunity and the level of technology maturity; it also represents an overview of the relative ease of commercialization and the market potential for key innovation areas. Innovation potential is huge in most segments and many are yielding double-digit growth.

Electronics 113

Table 9.1 Innovation Opportunities in the Electronics Industry

Area of Innovation	Current Market Size (2019) (in $ Billion)	CAGR Year (2019– 2035) (%)	Market Opportunity
Advanced display technology	28	13.0	• OLED • QLED • MicroLED (or µLED)
Flexible and stretchable electronics	22	7.7	• Stretchable circuits • Stretchable conductors • Stretchable batteries • Photovoltaics
Personal robots	9.5	11.9	• Entertainment & toy robots • Education robots • Security robots • Handicap assistance
Sensing technology	141	8.4	• Radar, lidar, ultrasonic sensor • Temperature/pressure sensor • Image and position sensor • Biosensor • Level and flow sensor • Motion sensor
Internet connectivity	385	9.1	• Broadband services • Wireless connectivity
Energy-efficient technologies	125	6.2	• Smart meter • Smart grid • Smart lighting • Connected appliances • Smart HVAC • LED lighting
Miniaturization of electronic devices	29	12.6	• MEMS technology • Inkjet heads • Microphones • Accelerometers • Gyroscopes • Digital compasses • Microbolometers • Micro displays
Big data	49	10.2	• Content management • Data warehousing • Data governance • Data analytics
Cloud computing	224	~17.0	• Software as a Service (SaaS) • Platform as a Service (PaaS) • Infrastructure as a Service (IaaS)

Source: Lucintel

114 Emerging Innovations by Industry

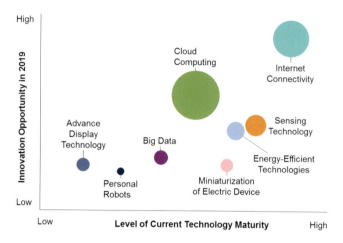

Figure 9.10 Level of Technology Maturity by Innovation Category in the Electronics Industry.
Note: Size of the Bubble Represents Market Size in 2035.
Source: Lucintel.

Cloud computing and sensing technology offer the greatest revenue growth potential. Internet connectivity and miniaturization of electronic devices are highly mature technologies. Advanced display technology and energy-efficient electronics provide relatively lower innovation opportunities but greater scope for commercialization success.

In terms of technological maturity, most segments require significant investment to develop commercial readiness. Smart cities, connected homes, and industrial IoT are more commercialized technology. Availability of low-cost sensors, proliferation of Wi-Fi, and artificial intelligence are leading technology.

Highlights

Advanced Display Technology: Companies such as **Samsung, Sony,** and LG are developing OLED capabilities for foldable devices. LG is developing TVs for sizes in the range of 55″ to 77″ whereas Samsung is focusing on utilizing OLED technology in foldable smartphones.

Personal Robots: Softbank Robotics has developed a humanoid robot named Pepper which can detect human emotions and gestures and react accordingly. Robots capable of taking pictures and sending them to owners' smartphones are being developed by **Mayfield Robotics** and **Asus**. Aibo, launched by **Sony Corporation**, can easily adapt itself to the atmosphere of a house. Asimo, launched by **Honda Motor Company, Ltd.**, can predict real-time movements and shift its center of gravity.

Launched by **UBTECH Robotics,** Lynx is the mobile version of Alexa. **Alexa,** launched by Amazon, is a home assistance device. Lynx helps with online shopping from Amazon by ordering products through simple voice commands given to the personal robot.

Big Data: Software companies such as **Tableau** develop software which can help make data visible to any device, including desktops and smartphones. **New Relic,** a software analytics company based in America, has come up with a product known as the **Insights Data Explorer** to make data interpretation easier. Database and analytics providers have developed **apps** that manage data more efficiently. A log analysis tool has been developed by **Splunk Enterprise** to monitor real-time consumer behavior and transactions, providing protection against security threats.

Horizon Planning Implications

To put these research findings in context, the chart below categorizes each opportunity area in terms of the Expanded Horizons Model[13] described in Chapter 1.

Definition of Each Innovation Type: Horizon 1 = Incremental, line extension, continuous improvement; **Horizon 2** = New to company or new to a sector; **Horizon 3** = Disruptive, new to the world (Table 9.2).

Most of these innovations can be successful in any horizon, depending upon the application.

Trends and indicators would suggest the following approach for those investing in the electronics industry:

- **Advanced Display Technology**[14]**:** With its high projected growth rate, Horizon 2 opportunities are great, although identifying untapped customer needs could lead to Horizon 3 endeavors. LED continues to be a major display technology trend and "mini LEDs" or "micro LEDs" are more revolutionary and set to compete with OLED.

Table 9.2 Horizon Planning Implications for the Electronics Industry

Area of Innovation	Horizon 1	Horizon 2	Horizon 3
Advanced display technology	Y	Y	Y
Flexible and stretchable electronics	Y	Y	Y
Personal robots	Y	Y	Y
Sensing technology	Y	Y	Y
Energy-efficient technologies	Y	Y	Y
Internet connectivity	Y	Y	
Miniaturization of electronic devices	Y	Y	Y
Big data	Y	Y	Y
Cloud computing	Y	Y	Y

Source: **Innovation**edge, LLC.
Content Source: Lucintel

- **Personal Robots[15]:** This area has seen one of the highest future growth rates, making it suitable as a core or incremental activity. Innovations in the field of artificial intelligence have helped to create more user-friendly personal robots. **Horizons 1 and/or 2 are suitable**, although identifying untapped customer needs could lead to Horizon 3 endeavors.
- **Flexible and Stretchable Displays[16]:** With its high disruptive potential and projected growth rate, Horizons 2 and 3 opportunities are great. This category can be a launchpad for game-changing devices that give patients more connection and control. **Horizon 3 suggested.**
- **Sensing Technology[17, 18, 19]:** Within this category, promising technologies such as **radar** and **lidar** present Horizon 3 potential. Radar and lidar sensors support various new technologies of advanced driver assistance systems, such as automatic emergency-braking systems, adaptive cruise control, parking assistance systems, and night vision systems. **Horizons 1, 2, and/or 3 suggested.**
- **Energy-Efficient Technologies[20]:** Within this category, promising technologies such as **smart lighting, smart meters, and smart grids** present Horizon 3 potential. * **Horizons 1, 2, and/or 3 suggested.**
- **Internet Connectivity[21, 22]:** High-performance PCBs, smart antennas, and power amplifiers are already prevalent and show no signs of slowing down. **Horizon 2 or 3 suggested.**
- **Miniaturization of Electronic Devices:** Within this category, miniaturization in sensors, ECUs, and other electronic component leads to the widespread adoption of many new technologies. **Horizon 1, 2 or 3 suggested.**
- **Big Data:** Advances in big data technology will increase adoption in various industries such as the healthcare, banking, and insurance sectors. **Horizons 1, 2, and/or 3 suggested.**
- **Cloud Computing:** This area has the largest opportunities and highest future growth rate, making it suitable as a core or incremental activity. This category is a solid one with potential breakthroughs in the field of public, private, and hybrid cloud areas. * **Horizons 1, 2, and/or 3 suggested.**

As per our study, it's quite clear that the nine key opportunity areas in the electronics industry all hold high growth potential as the overall industry continues to expand. The megatrends of increasing population, high disposable income, automation, growing use of electronics devices in daily life, and ease in lifestyle make this industry ripe for innovation, both short and long term. These opportunities are further accelerated by the push for touchless products and services in the COVID-19 era.

References

1. Lucintel publication, Strategic technology trends in the Global OLED Display Market, 2021.
2. "New LG home entertainment company CEO reveals business strategies for 2015", *LG Electronics (LG)*, Jan. 07, 2015.
3. Rick Nelson, "Heterogeneous integration boosts sensor systems", *Gale Academic*, Sep., 2016.
4. Lucintel publication, Growth Opportunities in the Global Flexible Printed Circuit Board Market Analysis, 2020.
5. Lucintel publication, Cleaning Robot Market Report: Trends, Forecast and Competitive Analysis, 2021.
6. Lucintel publication, Opportunities in the Sensor Market: Growth Trends, Forecast and Competitive Analysis, 2020.
7. Lucintel publication, Opportunities and Competitive Analysis of the Radar Sensor Market, 2021.
8. Lucintel publication, Growth Opportunities in the Global Lidar Market, 2021.
9. Lucintel publication, Trends, Opportunities and Competitive Analysis of the MEMS Gyroscope Market, 2021.
10. Roberto V. Zicari, "Managing big data. An interview with David Gorbet", *ODBMS Industry Watch*, Jul. 02, 2012.
11. "Interview with Michel CUI from Alibaba Cloud Europe", *Blumorpho*, Jul. 02, 2018.
12. "High-density interconnects: Enabling the intelligence of things", *The PCB Magazine*, Apr., 2015.
13. **Innovation**edge, LLC., Expanded Horizons Model ©
14. Lucintel publication, Opportunities in the Micro LED Market: Growth Trends, Forecast and Competitive Analysis, 2020.
15. Lucintel publication, Opportunities in the Artificial Intelligence Market: Market size, Trends and Growth Analysis, 2020.
16. Lucintel publication, Technology Trends in the Global Flexible Display Market, 2021.
17. Lucintel publication, Opportunities and Competitive Analysis of the Image Sensor Market, 2021.
18. Lucintel publication, Growth Opportunities in the Global Position Sensor Market, 2021.
19. Lucintel publication, Opportunities in the Biosensor market: Market size, Trends and Growth Analysis, 2021.
20. Lucintel publication, Outdoor LED Lighting Market Report: Trends, Forecast and Competitive Analysis, 2021.
21. Lucintel publication, Opportunities in the Wireless Sensor Market: Market size, Trends and Growth Analysis, 2021.
22. Lucintel publication, Wireless Connectivity Market Report: Trends, Forecast and Competitive Analysis, 2021.

Chapter 10

Internet of Things (IoT)

In this chapter, we consider the following aspects of the Internet of Things (IoT) industry:

- Emerging Innovations
- Revenue Impact and Resulting Growth Opportunities
- Horizon Planning Implications

Emerging Innovations

The IoT is one of the greatest innovations of our time, significantly contributing to new business models, connected products/services, and improved quality of life. Our observation is that with emerging innovations in sensors, artificial intelligence (AI), and machine learning, IoT is creating value by enhancing customer experience as well as creating new markets. AI and sensors are big enablers in the development of IoT devices/machines. In IoT, sensors allow the collection of a vast amount of data, whereas AI helps in processing the data and developing smarter applications/systems. AI-enabled IoT creates intelligent machines that support decision-making with little or no human interference. One can consider IoT devices as the body/digital system while AI as the brain of a system. Thus, in all IoT applications, sensors are used to collect vast amounts of operational and environmental data to be sorted, analyzed, and turned into actionable insights by AI. The **biggest applications** for IoT are **connected homes, connected wearables, connected cars, smart cities,** and the **industrial internet. Smart cities, connected homes,** and **connected cars** are the **most disruptive** innovation areas, and **connected wearables** offer the **highest future growth rate** during the forecast period.

In the above IoT applications, there will be greater usage of AI and sensors in future to make devices/machines behave smarter. With the increase in data collection in all IoT devices, there is increasing data traffic across applications and industries, which leads the need for the 5G networks to cater to the growing needs for data speed, reliability,

DOI: 10.4324/9781003177906-14

and low latency; 5G comes with enormous benefits such as lower latency, faster speeds, and greater load capacity. Some researchers believe that in real-world conditions 5G could deliver browsing and downloading speeds more than 20 times faster than the 4G network. For example, a 2-hour movie can be downloaded in less than 10 seconds with 5G vs. about 6 minutes with 4G. Thus, 5G technology will boost performance of industrial IoT, smart cities, connected cars, connected homes, and connected energy projects.

Kevin Wen, President of D-Link Europe, says, "The average household will have more and more IoT gadgets in the coming year. Some consumers won't even be aware that the devices they own are 'connected', such as an energy management device from their utility company. But eventually everything in the home will move to become digital, Internet-connected devices."[1] Increasing technological development will transform the life of disabled people. Wearable cameras will be introduced which can read sign language, detect faces and obstacles, and speak through an earpiece. Advanced earpieces will be developed which can filter out and amplify sounds for enhanced hearing. Virtual assistants built into contact lenses, for example, can perceive emotional reactions, predict thoughts and intentions, and enable the wearer to react accordingly. They can also improve vision and help diagnose medical conditions.

Augmented reality is likely to enhance the shopping experience. An interactive mirror can help buyers select clothing by providing an image of how an outfit will look as well as offering intelligently selected alternatives. Overall, the increasing penetration of Wi-Fi and the reduced cost of sensor technology are positively affecting innovation in the IoT market.

In Figure 10.1, we are presenting a broad categorization of the top innovation initiatives in the IoT industry:

Connected homes are the result of tremendous growth in internet connectivity, which has given rise to new applications of communication and information technology. Today, a connected home has automated air temperature control, lighting, locks, and entertainment. Future connected homes will be smarter and safer and will offer more convenience. There will be more energy-efficient homes, which might even generate energy and use water more efficiently. Bathrooms of the future will be self-cleaning based on technologies used by aircraft manufacturers, such as Boeing, for self-cleaning cabin toilets. Smart security devices that support 24/7 home monitoring will continue to gain popularity, along with smart refrigerators, air conditioners, washing machines, window treatments, lighting, and televisions that allow remote access and control of settings. Other than these, Kevin Wen, President of D-Link Europe, commented, "there is huge demand for security products as people realize the benefits of being able to keep an eye on their property, their pets

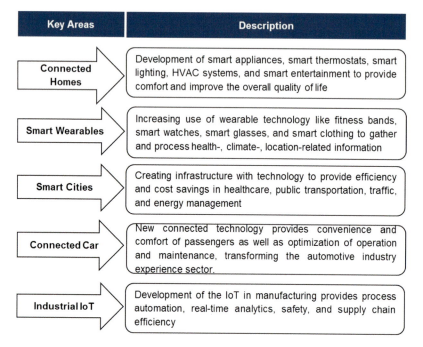

Figure 10.1 Key Innovation Areas for the IoT Market.
Source: Lucintel.

or families from wherever they are. Being able to access a live video feed from the monitor that users can view from their mobile devices is really appealing."[1] In the future, energy management and sensors will be at the top of the agenda. This has already happened in the United States, but in Europe the market is slightly behind in adoption.

We find that there are significant new opportunities emerging for consumer electronics companies as a result of connected homes to provide homeowners with comfort, security, energy efficiency, and convenience benefits (Figure 10.2).

Home security and surveillance systems are essential features of a smart home. Lighting control devices allow homeowners to track motion, occupancy, and temperature, and human motion detection information is built in for automated lighting. Christopher Zenaty, VP Sales Hikvision, said,

> In the video surveillance market, the behavioural analytic products coming out in the market today ensures that video will have tremendous value not only for criminal identification but for the retail marketing side. If you are a major retail chain and you want to

Figure 10.2 Innovation Areas in IoT for Connected Homes.

track the behavioural tendencies of your customers or break down demographics by age, gender or race, along with seeing where shoppers migrate to when on the retail floor and what draws them in, this will evolve into an incredibly useful tool across myriad market sectors.[2]

Technology giants like **Google** (Google Home), **Amazon** (Amazon Echo), **Microsoft** (Lab of Things), and **Tesla** (smart wall and solar tiles) are researching and heavily investing in smart home products. **Honeywell, Johnson & Johnson, ADT Corporation, Control4 Corporation, United Technologies Corporation, Siemens AG, Philips, Acuity Brands,** and **Vivint Inc.** are the major players in this market.

Utilities are critical to the success of building smarter cities across the region – and the country. As per Mike Zeto, General Manager and Executive Director, Smart Cities, AT&T, "smart cities framework brings together utilities, economic development organizations, research institutions, tech companies, the developer community and, of course, the cities themselves. This helps drive real value to cities and their citizens."[3] **Smart cities** are the combination of intelligent mobility, smart security, smart energy, smart infrastructure, smart education, and smart healthcare. Areas of focus include the development of highly advanced waste management systems, parking assistance applications, open data sharing for displaying information (such as air quality or hygiene ratings), bacteria-free touchscreens for information display, and crisis-alert/response systems. Companies are also focusing on renewable resources (such as solar panels), water recycling systems, and climate control systems. Leaders include **Huawei Investment & Holding Co., Ltd., Cisco Systems, IBM Corporation, Microsoft Corporation, Oracle Corporation, Schneider Electric, Siemens AG, Ericsson, Hitachi Ltd.,** and **Toshiba Corporation** (Figure 10.3).

Figure 10.3 Innovation Areas in IoT for Smart Cities.

During our study we found that **connected wearables** are growing at double digits and gaining prominence as they provide real-time health monitoring. Wearable technology increased in popularity with the advent of the Bluetooth headset in 2002. As commented by Kevin Wen, President of D-Link Europe, "During the last two to three years, wearable devices become a part of the smart home ecosystem, allowing people to remotely switch smart home appliances on or off via their smart watch, as well as a mobile or tablet."[1] The iconic wearable technology devices **Nike+, Fitbit, and Google Glass** were introduced between 2006 and 2013, but 2014 was the banner year for wearable technology. In that year, activity trackers became popular and the Apple Watch was introduced. Now there are wearable devices for hundreds of applications. Wristbands are available that monitor blood oxygen wirelessly. Healthcare professionals and patients are using smart patches for remote monitoring and home diagnosis. Tattoo-like plastic patches that monitor vital signs and smart contact lenses that can monitor blood sugar levels have become popular during the past five years.

Paul Marushka, President and CEO of Sphera Solutions, said, "wearables, which harness the power of the rapidly expanding Internet of Things technology, clearly offer more opportunity for major advancements in workplace safety than we have seen in decades."[4] The future of wearable devices, which includes activity trackers, smart watches, smart

Figure 10.4 Innovation Areas in IoT for Connected Wearables.

glasses, and embedded sensors in clothing, is continuously evolving with technological advances and new products. There are more and more sophisticated digital wearable fitness gadgets that wirelessly measure real-time health data. Major technology brands like **Fitbit** and **Apple** continue to focus on R&D in this area (Figure 10.4).

Digital fitness devices are portable wearable devices which continuously measure real-time fitness, heart rate, sleep patterns, calorie consumption, and other statistics. They provide valuable health insights, ranging from physical activity to stress levels to emotional state. While compact in nature, they offer superior performance. They have a long battery life and make use of special single-printed circuit boards which consume less power. The smart sensors used in these devices provide precise data. They are compatible with all types of operating systems. Gregory Moore, Vice President, Healthcare, of Google Cloud stated,

> At Google, our vision is to transform the way health information is organized and made useful. By enabling Fitbit to connect and manage key health and fitness data using our Google Cloud Healthcare API, we are getting one step closer to this goal. Together, we have the opportunity to deliver up-to-date information to providers, enhancing their ability to follow and manage the health of their patients and guide their treatment.[5]

Connected cars offer several features including infotainment systems, navigation systems, and safety and diagnostic systems. Automotive original equipment manufacturers (OEMs) are developing a variety of new technologies that will make cars far more digitally connected than they are now; for example, navigation systems will provide the fastest route to the driver. Cars are currently equipped with vehicle management systems which provide detailed performance data that can be shared with insurance companies and fleet owners. To reduce accidents, anti-fatigue devices can monitor drivers' vital functions and alert them of potential

Figure 10.5 Innovation Areas in IoT for Connected Cars.

problems. In the future, connected cars could also make payments for road tolls, insurance, servicing, car rentals, and other expenses. **Connected cars** are also expected to offer Wi-Fi and LTE data connections for their passengers. Vehicle-to-vehicle (V2V) and vehicle-to-infrastructure (V2I) systems are being developed for better traffic management and accident avoidance. In the future, connected cars are expected to inform drivers of tourist coupons and other travel offers in different cities. **Technologically advanced products such as GPS, parking assistance systems, and traffic sign recognition are anticipated to boost the connected car market** (Figure 10.5).

The **industrial IoT** has the potential to transform businesses. The industrial IoT is required for automation, smart manufacturing, and digital supply chain management. It also provides operational efficiency, connectivity, scalability, time savings, and cost savings. Thus, many companies are using industrial IoT to achieve higher productivity and performance.

Specifically, companies are turning to technological solutions such as **robots, cloud computing,** and **sensors**. Companies are saving costs as a result of predictive maintenance, improved safety, and other operational efficiencies. Smart sensors and other IoT technologies are monitoring how products are handled during transport and across the supply chain. For example, Jack Levis, Senior Director of Process Management, UPS, said,

> By using IoT and predictive analytics, UPS has ultimately been able to better control and manage its assets, which has led to significant benefits. Combining knowledge of a given day's delivery locations, which packages are in which warehouses, truck locations and real-time traffic information allows UPS to optimize its routes. With IoT technology, UPS has cut the miles driven per year by 100

Internet of Things (IoT) 125

Figure 10.6 Innovation Areas in Industrial IoT.

million, ultimately cutting CO2 emissions by 100,000 metric tons, using 10 million fewer gallons of fuel and saving the company $350 million to $400 million per year.[6]

As per our research we find that **technologically advanced products such as robotics and smart automation solutions are anticipated to boost the industrial IoT market** (Figure 10.6).

Revenue Impact and Resulting Growth Opportunities

To summarize our study, connected wearables offer the highest growth opportunity during the forecast period, whereas smart cities are the largest current opportunity where companies have significantly invested to mature the technology. With the right strategies, companies can realize significant opportunities in connected home, connected health, connected cars, smart cities, and industrial IoT.

Although the COVID-19 pandemic has affected the growth of various industries, the immediate impact of outbreak is varied as well. Some of the industries will register a drop in demand and some of them will unlock new growth opportunities; IoT is one of the industries which holds a promising future despite the pandemic. The COVID outbreak has had an impact on psychology and consumer sentiments and thus created the need for a touchless economy, which will allow the growth of industry 4.0, smart homes, IoTs, and AI. We are expecting a shift toward flexible and smart manufacturing, which can help part fabricators maintain a balance between their inventory and actual demand. During the post-COVID period, there will be a significant increase in digital transformations in payments, receipts, supply chains, and many other aspects of business to increase efficiency. Companies that have already invested in smart manufacturing or contactless technologies will be doing more to improve production efficiencies as well as workers' safety to avoid further transmission of the virus. Major manufacturers such as Boeing, Airbus, Safran, Honeywell, GE Aviation, General Motors, and Ford have already invested in smart manufacturing or contactless technologies to realize reductions in costs, wastage, and production time.

Table 10.1 shows the market size and growth rate for key innovation opportunity areas.

Our study says that innovations in connected homes, connected wearables, smart cities, and connected cars offer high degrees of disruption. In connected cars, advanced driver assistance systems (ADAS) are currently available, but mostly in high- and medium-end cars. Innovation leading to cost reduction of this technology will create huge opportunities, making it feasible for low-cost cars as well.

In terms of technological maturity, most segments still require significant investment. Smart cities, connected homes, and industrial IoT are the more commercialized segments at this point. Availability of low-cost sensors, proliferation of Wi-Fi, and AI are leading technologies. Competitive intensity is low to moderate in most segments due to limited number of players and rapid growth in these areas.

Specifically, here's an overview of the relative ease of commercialization and market potential for key innovation areas (Figure 10.7).

Innovation in **smart cities** and **connected homes** offer great opportunity. Both are highly commercialized with good levels of technology maturity and confidence. **Connected wearables** and **connected cars** are currently small markets, but both have good potential for commercialization success as the maturity level is still low. **Industrial IoT** has strong future innovation opportunity though this technology is currently at a relatively lower commercialization level.

Internet of Things (IoT)   127

Table 10.1 Innovation Opportunities in the IoT Market

Area of Innovation	Current Market Size (2019) (in $ Billion)	CAGR Year (2019–2035) (%)	Market Opportunity
Connected homes	74	7.6	• Connected appliances • Connected thermostats • Smart lighting • Smart entertainment • Connected locks, video surveillance • Fire sprinklers and extinguishers • Intruder alarms
Connected wearables	41	11.2	• Smart watches • Fitness bands • Wearable fabrics • Smart glasses • Action cameras
Smart cities	509	11.3	• Smart meters • Smart traffic lights • Smart parking • Electric vehicle charging stations
Connected cars	62	18.4	• Passenger safety • Vehicle diagnostic • Infotainment and navigation • Fleet management
Industrial IoT	64	7.2	• Fleet and asset tracking • Machine-to-machine (M2M) control applications • Robotics • Vibration and wear and tear analysis • Auto-diagnosis

Source: Lucintel

Highlights

Below are summaries of IoT innovation activities in selected key innovation areas:

Connected Homes[7]: **ADT, Robert Bosch, Vivint,** and **Honeywell** are developing technologies to manufacture connected devices. ADT launched the ADT Pulse app. Through this app, subscribers turn on

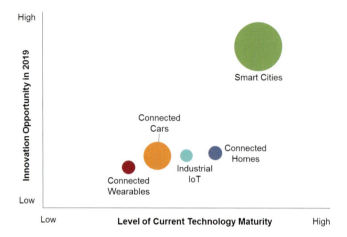

Figure 10.7 Level of Technology Maturity by Innovation Category in the IoT Market.
Note: Size of the Bubble Represents Market Size in 2035.
Source: Lucintel.

lights, monitor carbon monoxide, arm alarms, and even control heating with their voice. Honeywell launched Tuxedo Touch, the touchscreen security and home automation controller that can serve as the central hub of a connected home or business.

Connected Wearables[8, 9]: **Omron, Fitbit, Apple,** and **Medtronic** are developing technologies to manufacture connected wearable devices. Medtronic launched the **Guardian Connect** system, a continuous glucose-monitoring system that can alert patients to a high- or low-sugar glucose event. Fitbit launched its Alta range that tracks all-day activity, and features auto-sleep tracking, move reminders, a clock, smart track tag display, and accessory bands.

Connected Cars: Companies such as **Google, Tesla,** and **Volkswagen** are developing disruptive technologies to further advance autonomous vehicles. Google has started small-scale deployment of low-speed L5 self-driving vehicles in campus-like environments and cities; Volkswagen has launched Sedric with full Level 5 autonomy.

Other major areas of innovation are smart cities and industrial IoT. **Schneider, ABB, GE, IBM,** and **Cisco** are some of the leading players operating in these markets.

Horizon Planning Implications

To put these research findings in context, the chart below categorizes each opportunity area in terms of the Expanded Horizons Model[10] described in Chapter 1.

Internet of Things (IoT)   129

Table 10.2 Horizon Planning Implications for the IoT Industry

Area of Innovation	Horizon 1	Horizon 2	Horizon 3
Connected homes	Y	Y	Y
Connected wearables	Y	Y	Y
Smart cities	Y	Y	Y
Connected cars	Y	Y	Y
Industrial IoT	Y	Y	Y

Source: **Innovation**edge, LLC.
Content Source: Lucintel

Definition of Each Innovation Type: Horizon 1 = Incremental, line extension, continuous improvement; **Horizon 2** = New to company or new to a sector; **Horizon 3** = Disruptive, new to world (Table 10.2).

Most of the innovations can be categorized as Horizons 1, 2, or 3. Trends and indicators would suggest the following approach for those investing in IoT development:

- **Connected Homes**[11, 12]: With their high disruptive potential and projected growth rate, Horizon 2 and 3 opportunities are great. Advances in sensors, AI technology, and cloud-based technology have the potential for creating breakthrough products with customizable benefits. **Horizons 1, 2, and/or 3 suggested.**
- **Connected Wearables**[13]: Wearables also have high disruptive potential and growth projected over the forecast period. This category can be a launchpad for game-changing devices that provide continuous feedback to users and monitor activities such as number of steps, exercise, sleep, or nutrition. **Horizons 1, 2, and/or 3 suggested.**
- **Smart Cities**[14, 15, 16]: This area has the largest current opportunity as well as technological maturity, making it suitable as a core or incremental activity. Within this category, promising application areas like **intelligent transportation, smart public security, smart healthcare,** and **smart energy** present Horizon 3 potential. **Horizons 1, 2, and/or 3 suggested.**
- **Connected Cars**[17]: Within this category, promising technologies such as **GPS, vehicle management, and driver assistance** present Horizon 3 potential. **Horizons 1, 2, and/or 3 suggested.**
- **Industrial IoT**[18]: Within this category, promising technologies such as **robotics** and **smart automation solutions** present Horizon 3 potential. **Horizons 1, 2, and/or 3 suggested.**

References

1. Sam Pudwell, "Interview: Consumer demands on smart home technology", *ITProPortal*, Oct. 07, 2015.

2. Steve Lasky, "Disruption and innovation are separated by a fine line", *Security Infowatch*, Nov. 10, 2017.
3. "AT&T, current, Georgia power and the city of Atlanta light the way for smart city Innovation", *AT&T*, Jan. 31, 2017.
4. Andy Hosman, "How wearables could disrupt workplace safety", *EHS Today*, Jul. 07, 2017.
5. Ryan Daws, "Fitbit leverages Google Cloud to accelerate healthcare innovation", *IoT News*, Apr. 30, 2018.
6. "Intelligent world: The state of the IoT - Forbes insights eBook", *Forbes*, Jun. 12, 2018.
7. Lucintel publication, Trends, Opportunities and Competitive Analysis of the Global Home Security Market, 2020.
8. Lucintel publication, Wearable Technology Market Report: Trends, Forecast and Competitive Analysis, 2021.
9. Lucintel publication, Opportunities in the Smart Watch Market: Market size, Trends and Growth Analysis, 2021.
10. **Innovation**edge, LLC., Expanded Horizons Model ©
11. Lucintel publication, Growth Opportunities in the Global IoT Sensor Market, 2021.
12. Lucintel publication, Opportunities in the 5G IoT Sensor Market: Market size, Trends and Growth Analysis, 2021.
13. Lucintel publication, Opportunities and Competitive Analysis of the Global Digital Fitness Market, 2017.
14. Lucintel publication, Smart Traffic Management System Market Report: Trends, Forecast and Competitive Analysis, 2020.
15. Lucintel publication, Trends, Opportunities and Competitive Analysis of the Smart Parking Market, 2021.
16. Lucintel publication, Opportunities in the Electric Vehicle (EV) Charging Station Market: Growth Trends, Forecast and Competitive Analysis, 2021.
17. Lucintel publication, Opportunities in the Automotive Parking Assistance System Market: Growth Trends, Forecast and Competitive Analysis, 2020.
18. Lucintel publication, Growth Opportunities in the Global Smart Robot Market, 2021.

Chapter 11

Medical Devices

In this chapter, we consider the following aspects of the medical devices industry:

– Emerging Innovations
– Revenue Impact and Resulting Growth Opportunities
– Horizon Planning Implications

Emerging Innovations

The medical device industry is driven by innovation and technological developments. Powered by advances in technologies such as the Internet of Things (IoT), sensors, robots, electronics, batteries, and 3D printing, new and innovative medical devices are being introduced to healthcare facilities and patients' homes. Within the medical industry, we find that advanced diagnostic, monitoring, and surgical procedures are creating new markets/applications as well as demand for replacements and upgrades of older technologies as they become obsolete. Alex Gorsky, CEO of Johnson & Johnson, stated:

> I think the movement from a completely fee-for-service to one that focuses more on outcomes. And just as we've seen in our life where our iPhone, our iPad is converging into other areas, I think we're going to see the same thing in medical device technology in consumer and pharma in different ways. All of the instruments will be smart instruments by the way that they are integrated into the operating room and connected in a number of different ways.[1]

During our study we observed that manufacturers are currently focusing on accuracy, less pain, reduction of procedural time, and shorter hospital stays. **Minimally invasive surgery, robotics, and 3D printing** are

DOI: 10.4324/9781003177906-15

enabling better patient outcomes, and high demand for these surgical processes is driving further innovation[2, 3].

Major manufacturers are adopting **3D printing** technology in bio-printing, tissue engineering, and other advanced prosthetics. A fully functioning kidney created from the patient's own cells is just one example of breakthrough innovation under development. Overall 3D bio-printed human tissue prosthetics and 3D printing-based implants are becoming increasingly viable as materials technology advances. **Smart implants** and **advanced prosthetics** are the most disruptive innovation areas and smart implants offer the highest future growth rate during the forecast period.

Other key innovations are small, relatively low-cost **robotic systems** that allow high-precision surgery, **smart medical capsules** with miniaturized embedded electronics and personalized care enabled by **nanotechnology** and **genomics**[4].

Pressure to reduce healthcare expenditure while improving patient care combined with emerging technologies and an aging population is creating both opportunities and challenges. Since healthcare expenditure is correlated with increased usage of medical devices, the need to decrease the cost of devices is mounting. At the same time, increased expenditure is linked with higher demand. The challenge is getting the cost/profit ratio right.

Figure 11.1 represents a broad categorization of top innovation opportunities in the medical device industry.

Connected health strategies are creating new market opportunities for medical device manufacturers to shift from traditional to alternative technologies/methods. Digitalization and connectivity will help to realize a patient-centric approach, pulling together patient-specific monitoring, diagnosis, and treatment information. As per James Stansberry, Senior Vice President, Samsung Electronics,

> Device manufacturers will be able to deliver new benefits to their customers with growing need for connected health platforms. This is an incredibly exciting time in healthcare, as the industry begins to harness the power of data to bring better care to consumers.[5]

Connected health systems enable remote diagnoses, monitoring, and treatment by enabling access to patient-specific information from multiple sources. Digitalization and connectivity help realize today's emphasis on more efficient, patient-centric approaches while reducing cost, paperwork, and human error. They are especially helpful in monitoring and treating patients who are chronically ill, elderly, or housebound; the patient can be connected to a service network to assist in the case of emergencies as well. Finally, electronic health records (EHRs) allow

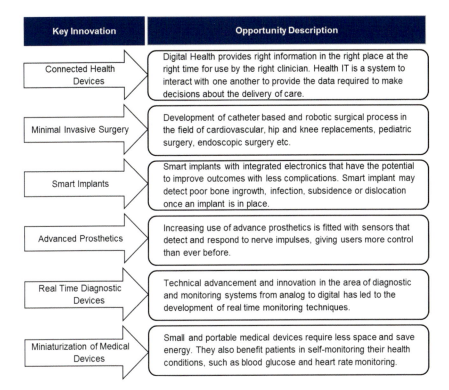

Figure 11.1 Key Innovation Opportunity Areas in Medical Devices.
Source: Lucintel.

doctors to pass along patient information to colleagues and specialists for consultation (Figure 11.2). Waqaas Al-Siddiq, CEO, Biotricity stated:

> For medical device manufacturers to successfully enter and establish themselves in the new connected healthcare industry, it is imperative that they look beyond traditional forms of technological innovation. IoT, for example, would be an avenue for consideration and medical device manufacturers are uniquely positioned to be successful in this market, as they have a profound understanding of the regulatory process, critical applications, and patient risk.[6]

Minimally invasive surgeries are gaining prominence as they reduce scarring, trauma, risk of infection, and blood loss while speeding recovery time and shortening length of hospital stays. "Minimally invasive surgery helps reduce pain, scarring and recovery time after surgery. The robotically-assisted surgical device (RASD) technology is a specialized

Figure 11.2 Innovation Areas in Connected Health Devices. (a) BPM Monitor; (b) Personal ECG.

innovation in minimally invasive surgery designed to enhance the surgeon's access and visualization within confined operative sites,"[7] as said by Binita Ashar, Director at the Surgical Devices Division of the FDA's Center for Devices and Radiological Health. Smaller incisions minimize pain and swelling. Yeung Chung-Kwong (Prof Yeung), Honorary Clinical Professor, Department of Surgery, the University of Hong Kong (HKU), commented: "It is our belief that by integrating cutting-edge technologies with the surgical robotic platform we can make future robotic surgery much safer and less invasive, thus providing significantly better care for our patients."[8] **Advanced techniques such as computer-aided surgery, robotics, and 3D printing are anticipated to boost the minimally invasive surgery market. Catheter-based robotic processes are becoming especially popular for cardiovascular surgery, hip and knee replacements, and pediatric surgery.** Overall, the applications and benefits of minimally invasive surgery are significant.

Within the healthcare industry, as per our analysis, smart implants/ medical implants are growing at double digits and creating new markets as well as a demand for the replacement of older implants. According to Prof. Eric Ledet, Rensselaer Polytechnic Institute,

> Smart implants have the potential to significantly impact the way we practice medicine. By enabling personalized medicine, each patient's treatment can be optimized. The key to this is economical and robust implantable sensors. For decades, this has been elusive. However, simple passive resonator-based sensors may be a viable option to bringing smart implant into daily clinical practice. Future sensors can theoretically be tuned to measure the presence or absence of specific chemicals, molecules, or biologics.[9]

An implanted chip can detect a patient's hormone level, blood glucose concentration, bacteria, electrical activity, and temperature, thus providing doctors with real-time biofeedback. Smart devices can be implanted in the brain, heart, and other body parts and can be used to treat and monitor epilepsy, Parkinson's disease, and orthopedic conditions.

Dr. Guido Grappiolo, a surgeon, said,

> Healthcare providers can improve patient outcomes significantly by developing smart implants. Patients equipped with smart implants, rather than conventionally manufactured ones, have a lower risk of getting a serious infection post-op, will suffer from less discomfort and pain, and could also be less likely to need revision surgeries in the future. In my opinion, 3D printed orthopaedic implants could last a lifetime, and with new innovations like smart implants on the horizon.[10]

Implants can also replace missing or damaged biological structures of the body. Medical implants include **orthopedic** (knee, spine, and hip), **cardiac** (pacemaker, coronary stent), and **neuro-stimulators** (spinal cord, sacral nerve, deep brain, vagus nerve).

One of the biggest healthcare challenges is engineering products to match nature. Current prostheses (artificial devices) are used to replace body parts which may have been lost through trauma, disease, or congenital conditions. Prosthetics are intended to restore the normal functions of the missing body part. Andy Miah, Director, Creative Futures Institute, said:

> Most of the human body is currently replaceable with artificial implants and advanced prosthetics. Mechanical organs, including the heart, lungs, pancreas, spleen, and kidneys, either currently exist or are in advanced stages of development. Many electronic implants, like pacemakers and hearing aids, already control, restore, or enhance normal body functions.[11]

Dean Kamen, Founder, Deka Research & Development, thinks that this area is going to see probably the biggest growth in the medical field over the next decade.

> We're trying to grow tissues, including skin and whole organs, like lungs and kidneys, and vascular structures, like fistulas. I think that the intersection of engineering, biology, and medicine allows things to be done that ten years ago would have been considered science fiction.[12]

Advanced prosthetics can interface directly with the human nervous system and organic tissue. Mind-controlled robotic hands/legs can simulate touch sensations in users' brains, enabling them to control the hand or leg as if it were their own.

Manufacturers are now focusing to develop lighter, smaller, better-controlled, more lifelike and affordable prosthetics. Advanced prosthetics include bionic hearts, bionic cells, bionic knees, bionic eyes, and bionic arms. These are prostheses which can be integrated with body tissues, including the nervous system. They are highly advanced and able to respond to commands from the central nervous system and can more closely replicate normal movement and functionality. Growth is being fueled by private and public investors.

3D printing is playing a key role for its role in cost-effective creation of functioning prosthetics. Innovations include 3D printed skin for burn victims, airway splints for infants, facial reconstruction parts for cancer patients, and more. Growth is fueled by private and public investors (Figure 11.3).

Advanced grid computed systems, cloud-based solutions, wearable devices, smart mobile, smart gadgets for diagnosis, and implantable biosensors are likely to emerge as key technology enablers for real-time diagnostic and monitoring device innovation.

> The implantable platform uses intelligent implants that will pull data such as early warning signs of infection, monitoring bone density, and material wear. This capability will enable doctors to remotely monitor the implant. Our belief is that the future of orthopaedics is moving from mechanics (materials sciences, geometry, etc.) to more electronics – the use of microelectronics sensor to drive sensor-assisted surgery and remote monitoring,[13]

as said by Jay Pierce, CEO of OrthoSensor.

Figure 11.3 Innovations in Advanced Prosthetics.

Medical Devices 137

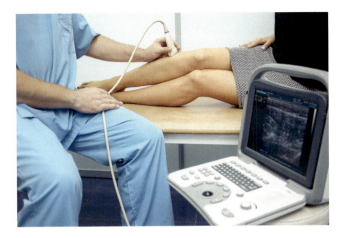

Figure 11.4 Miniaturization of Medical Devices.

Miniaturization is an important feature as today's medical devices are often hand-held and portable. Demand for comfort and convenience are growing to make the patient's experience easier. Compact, lightweight hand-held devices are suitable for clinical applications such as imaging internal organs. Francisco Almada Lobo, Chief Executive Officer and Co-Founder of Critical Manufacturing, said that "For the medical industry, miniature battery-powered sensor devices can be located near, attached to, or implanted in the body to monitor physiological signs. A new area of bioelectronics medicine is also emerging, facilitated by the miniaturization of electronics."[14] Windows PC-based architecture allows the packing of large amounts of processing power and intelligence into small devices. Portable and wearable devices are rapidly becoming the most common form of connected technology.

With improved quality, accuracy, reliability, flexibility, integration, functionality, and affordability, these smart devices will have an enormous and positive impact on healthcare delivery.

Revenue Impact and Resulting Growth Opportunities

Our research suggests that **smart implant and connected health devices** offer the **highest growth rate** during the forecast period, whereas **miniaturization** of medical devices offers the **largest opportunity to leverage mature technology**. Companies can realize significant opportunities in smart implants, connected health devices, advanced prosthetics,

138 Emerging Innovations by Industry

real-time diagnostics & monitoring, and miniaturization of medical devices with the right strategy.

In terms of impact of COVID, the healthcare industry has seen both positive and negative growth based on segments. Connected devices, home health, PPE kits, ventilators, and testing kits have witnessed a significant increase in demand during the pandemic. Majority of other type of surgeries, not related to COVID, have been given less priority during the pandemic, which resulted in the medical device market taking a backseat in some areas. We have also seen increased use of robots in hospitals. For example, a robot can allow healthcare workers to remotely take temperatures and measure blood pressure and oxygen saturation from patients hooked up to a ventilator. Robot can also disinfect hospitals, work space, and sensitive areas with ultraviolet light.

To more clearly show the market size and growth rate for key innovation opportunity areas, we've compiled Table 11.1.

It shows the market size and growth rate for key innovation opportunity areas.

Disruptive technologies can change the game for businesses, creating entirely new products and services, as well as shifting pools of value between producers and consumers.

Innovations in smart implants, minimally invasive surgery, prosthetics, and real-time diagnostic offer the high degrees of disruption. One of

Table 11.1 Innovation Opportunities in the Medical Device Industry

Area of Innovation	Market Size (2019) (in $ Billion)	CAGR Year (2019–2035) (%)	Market Opportunity
Connected health device	17	16.2	• Home healthcare • Remote patient monitoring
Minimal invasive and robotic surgery	39	7.4	• Robotic surgery • Catheter-based procedures
Smart implants/ medical implants	22	8.5	• Biosensors to microelectronic medical implants
Advanced prosthetics	2	9.6	• Robotic arm, legs
Real-time diagnostic and monitoring device	15	18.5	• Wearable healthcare devices
Miniaturization of medical devices	28	6.8	• Implantable device • Portable diagnostic devices

Source: Lucintel

the most potentially disruptive innovations is **smart probes** with smart scalpels that give hope to patients who have cancer. Due to their high precision and small size, they can be made tissue-selective in targeting cancerous cells, especially in nerves or vascular tissues. An Ireland-based company, Intelligent Implants, is among the first to develop smart implants with integrated electronics that have the potential to improve outcomes.

Though the innovation and disruption potential are great, the medical device industry faces strict compliance requirements from the government as well as companies' own standards of excellence. Such requirements span the supply chain and include materials usage, counterfeit parts, manufacturing procedures, and more. Regulatory compliance for miniaturization and real-time diagnostics is somewhat lower than for connected health devices, minimally invasive surgery, smart implants, and advanced prosthetics. However, stringent regulations mean the widespread use of certain new technologies will take time.

In terms of technological maturity, most segments require significant investment to develop commercial readiness. The speed of introduction of these new technologies depends not only on technical feasibility, but on acceptance by society. Ethics, perceived value to consumers, and longer-term ramifications must be considered. Competitive intensity is relatively low due to the presence of few players and high growth factors. In all, the potential rewards outweigh the risks.

Specifically, here's an overview of the relative ease of commercialization and market potential for key innovation areas (Figure 11.5).

Miniaturization offers the largest opportunity and is highly commercialized. Connected health devices offer the highest degree of technological maturity in a wide range of platforms. Smart implants and advanced prosthetics currently have lower technological maturity but future innovations will serve to close this gap. Minimally invasive surgery and real-time diagnostic & monitoring devices are in the growth stage of the innovation curve.

Highlights

Connected health device[15]**: Medtronic, Omron, Fitbit, and Roche Holding AG** are developing technologies to manufacture connected devices. Medtronic developed smart continuous glucose monitoring which alerts patients of potential high or low glucose events up to 60 minutes in advance. Omron developed the first single at-home BP monitoring device in the United States that measures blood pressure and EKG (electrocardiogram). The Fitbit fitness band provides pulse and heart rate tracking, multi-sports tracking, connected GPS, and cardio fitness level. Roche developed the equipped new spill-resistant smart pack and

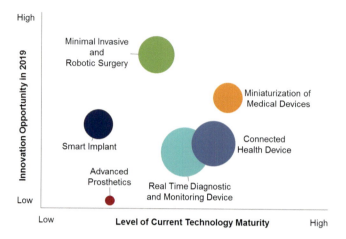

Figure 11.5 Level of Technology Maturity by Innovation Category in the Medical Device Industry.
Note: Size of the Bubble Represents Market Size in 2035.
Source: Lucintel.

wireless connectivity to mobile apps cloud-based diabetic management and remote monitoring.

Minimally invasive surgery[16, 17]: Laparoscopic surgery, robotic-assisted surgery, and catheter-based heart procedures are a few of the minimally invasive processes. For more than a decade, **Intuitive Surgical** has had a quasi-monopoly on the field of minimally invasive robotic surgery, but newcomers like **Cambridge Medical Robotics** and **TransEnterix** are now entering the market. Medtronic has made two major moves into surgical robotics: its acquisition of **COVIDien** for $50 billion and its emergence as **Mazor Robotics'** lead investor. **Medtronic-COVIDien** owns an extensive patent portfolio in the surgical robotics field.

Smart Implants[18, 19]: An Ireland-based company **Intelligent Implants** is one of the first to develop smart implants with integrated electronics. **Smart implants** is based on electrical stimulation techniques which can lead to bone cell proliferation. **Intelligent Implants** has incorporated a miniature electrical stimulation device into the standard PEEK (polyetheretherketone) cages, which are biocompatible materials implanted as spacers between vertebrae during spinal surgery. The most important part of the system is that it can increase fusion rates significantly in a safe and controlled fashion while accelerating healing. It can also monitor the formation of bone at the fusion site, gather and organize the data from monitoring the fusion process, and present it to caregivers and patients in an attractive way.

Other major areas of innovation are advanced prosthetics, real-time diagnostic & monitoring, and miniaturization of medical devices. **Siemens, GE Healthcare, Philips Healthcare, Toshiba, Otto Bock Inc., DJO Global Inc., Ossur Corporate, Ekso Bionics, Rex Bionics Ltd., Alter G, ReWalk Robotics** are some of the leading players operating in the real-time diagnostic & monitoring, smart implants, and advanced prosthetics market.

Horizon Planning Implications

To put these research findings in context, the chart below categorizes each opportunity area in terms of the Expanded Horizons Model[20] described in Chapter 1.

Definition of Each Innovation Type: Horizon 1 = Incremental, line extension, continuous improvement; **Horizon 2** = New to company or new to a sector; **Horizon 3** = Disruptive, new to the world (Table 11.2).

Most of the opportunities can be categorized as Horizons 1, 2, and 3. Trends and indicators would suggest the following approach for those investing in medical device development:

- **Connected Health**[21]: This area has the largest current opportunity as well as technological maturity, making it suitable as a core or incremental activity. The pervasiveness of connected systems among mainstream users suggests consumer wellness and tracking devices have the biggest but most competitive market. Cloud-based technology and apps are much the same. **Horizons 1 and/or 2 are suitable,** though identifying untapped customer needs could lead to Horizon 3 endeavors.
- **Minimally Invasive and Robotic Surgery:** Within this category, promising technologies such as **narrow band imaging endoscopes, confocal micro endoscopes,** and **HD cameras** for endoscopes, and **sensor technologies** such as **haptics** present Horizon 3 potential. **Horizons 1, 2, and/or 3 suggested.**

Table 11.2 Horizon Planning Implications for the IoT Industry

Area of Innovation	Horizon 1	Horizon 2	Horizon 3
Connected health devices	Y		
Minimally invasive surgery	Y	Y	Y
Smart implants	Y	Y	Y
Advanced prosthetics	Y	Y	Y
Real-time diagnostic and monitoring devices	Y	Y	Y
Miniaturization/portability	Y	Y	Y

Source: **Innovation**edge, LLC.
Content Source: Lucintel

- **Smart Implants:** With its high disruptive potential and projected growth rate, Horizons 2 and 3 opportunities are great. In particular, advances in sensor technology and miniaturization have the potential for creating breakthrough products with customizable and preventive benefits. **Horizon 2 or 3 suggested.**
- **Advanced Prosthetics:** Also disruptive, this category can be a launchpad for game-changing devices that give patients more connection and control. **Horizon 2 or 3 suggested.**
- **Real-Time Diagnostic and Monitoring Devices:** Along with connected health and smart implants, the ability to detect, monitor, and potentially prevent serious consequences in real time is becoming a must for all medical devices. This category is a solid one with potential breakthroughs in advanced grid systems, **cloud-based solutions, wearable devices, smart mobile, smart gadgets for diagnosis, and implantable biosensors. Horizon 1 or 2 suggested.**
- **Miniaturization/Portability:** Hand-held and portable devices are already prevalent and the trend shows no signs of slowing down. **Horizon 1 or 2 suggested.**

The six key opportunity areas in the medical device industry all hold high growth potential as the overall industry continues to expand. The megatrends of aging population, healthcare reform, emphasis on prevention, and early diagnosis combined with accelerated technology development make this industry ripe for innovation both in the short and in the long term.

References

1. Dave Schatz, "Johnson & Johnson to acquire medical device maker NeuWave", *New Brunswick Today*, Mar. 14, 2016.
2. Lucintel publication, Growth Opportunities in the Global 3D Printing Medical Device Market, 2021.
3. Lucintel publication, Opportunities in the Tissue Engineering Market: Market size, Trends and Growth Analysis, 2021.
4. Lucintel publication, Genomics Market Report: Trends, Forecast and Competitive Analysis, 2021.
5. Joost Maltha, "Philips and Samsung team up to expand the connected health ecosystem", *Philips*, Mar. 08, 2018.
6. HITC Staff, "AT&T Taps biotricity to power IoT wearable medical devices", *HIT Consultant*, Aug. 09, 2016.
7. "FDA clears new robotically-assisted surgical device for adult patients", *U.S. Food and Drug Administration*, Oct. 13, 2017.
8. "The world's first internally motorized minimally invasive surgical robotic system for single incision or natural orifice (incision-less) robotic surgery", *The University of Hong Kong (HKU)*, Mar. 02, 2016.
9. Mark Crawford, "Implantable sensors make medical implants smarter", *The American Society of Mechanical Engineers*, Sep. 05, 2013.

Medical Devices **143**

10. "3D-printed joints & implants: 100,000 patients later, The 3D-printed hip is a decade old and going strong", *GE Additive*, Mar. 05, 2018.
11. "Advances in prosthetics", *Science Blog*, Mar. 07, 2014.
12. Chau Tu, "A look into the future with Dean Kamen", *Science Friday*, Aug. 29, 2016.
13. "Real-time diagnostics for orthopedic implants", *HospiMedica International*, Aug. 08, 2011.
14. "Industry 4.0- manufacturing and the future of medical things", *Asian Hospital & Healthcare Management*.
15. Lucintel publication, Trends, Opportunities and Competitive Analysis of the Global Connected Health Device Market, 2020.
16. Lucintel publication, Opportunities and Competitive Analysis of the Minimally Invasive Surgical Instrument Market, 2021.
17. Lucintel publication, Top Technology Trends Reshaping Robotics Prosthetic Market, 2020.
18. Lucintel publication, Opportunities in the Interventional Cardiology and Peripheral Vascular Device Market: Growth Trends, Forecast and Competitive Analysis, 2020.
19. Lucintel publication, Technology Landscape, Trends and Opportunities in the Global Prosthetic Market, 2021.
20. **Innovation**edge, LLC., Expanded Horizons Model ©
21. Lucintel publication, Growth Opportunities in the Global Diagnostic Imaging Market, 2020.

Section III

Executing Your Strategy – Integrating Core Capabilities with External Opportunities

While innovation is key to business growth, it is clearly easier said than done. According to *Forbes*, nearly 90% of new product or service launches fail. This is not necessarily bad – failure means a company is taking risks. The intent of this book is not to eliminate risks and failures; it is to help you balance less risky core activities with bigger bets for revolutionary, yet sustainable growth. We have shared strategic insights, emerging innovation forecasts, and the **Innovation**edge **Growth Opportunity Framework** (IGOF)[1] to help you build your short- and long-term roadmap.

Chapter 12 summarizes key success factors and highlights the top 14 innovation areas across seven industries. The **Conclusion** recaps decision-making questions to ask yourself and offers specific action steps. This chapter also includes templates to facilitate opportunity valuation and comparison.

Reference

1. **Innovation**edge, LLC., **Innovation**edge Growth Opportunity Framework™.

DOI: 10.4324/9781003177906-16

Chapter 12

Summary

This book has presented numerous strategic insights and action steps as well as descriptions, forecasts, and projections for emerging innovations across seven key industries. The critical success factors and high potential growth opportunities are summarized below.

Critical Success Factors

1. Plan for Long- and Short-term Growth

    Experience has shown that having an innovation strategy across **three horizons** is the most effective way to protect your current business while creating the future. We define these horizons in **Innovation**edge, LLC's Expanded Horizons Model[1] as:

    -   Horizon 1 (H1) = Incremental, line extension, continuous improvement
    -   Horizon 2 (H2) = New to company or new to a sector
    -   Horizon 3 (H3) = Disruptive, new to the world

    Your organization's innovation ambition will guide your investment and resource allocation decisions. For long-term growth, invest more in Horizons 2 and 3 and provide ongoing support. Chapter 1 discusses resource allocation ratios, staffing, and organizational structures to align with your objectives. Chapters 5–11 frame innovation opportunities and technologies in the Expanded Horizons Model[1] context.

2. Leverage Core Strengths and Capabilities

    The next success factor is continuous development of **core capabilities and strengths.** In Chapter 2 we have outlined our Capabilities Advancement approach to ensure your company's competitiveness in an increasingly digital world (Figure 12.1).

3. Manage External Collaborations, Alliances, and Acquisitions

    The third factor is going outside your own four walls to accelerate innovation and growth. **Strategic partnerships, alliances, outsourcing, acquisitions,** and **networks** enable your organization to add new

DOI: 10.4324/9781003177906-17

148 Executing Your Strategy

Figure 12.1 Capabilities Advancement Approach for Increasing Company's Competitiveness.
Source: **Innovation**edge, LLC.

competencies as well as technologies and market access. The challenge is finding and choosing the right ones for your specific needs. Chapter 3 offers a discovery process to identify the best fit(s). Cultural alignment and its importance are also discussed. Chapters 5–11 list leading solution providers to help you scout potential partners.

4. Tap into Megatrends

The fourth factor is the future direction of markets, economies, technologies, and the world at large. Chapter 4 describes **seven major megatrends** that will impact innovation over the next 25–30 years. As mentioned previously, COVID-19 has spurred a number of significant megatrends, particularly in healthcare, medical devices, and automation. In combination with your company's goals and customer insights, understanding the future will tell you "where to play" so your company can win.

High Potential Growth Opportunities

Chapters 5–11 provide detailed information on revenue and growth potential, technology maturity, ecosystem/partner potential, and horizon suitability of emerging innovations across seven major industries. Of the more than 60 innovations discussed, 14 have the combined potential to reach approximately $10 trillion total by 2035 from $2 trillion total in 2019.

These high-potential opportunities are **smart cities, powertrain advancement, electric cars, sensing technologies, safety & security,**

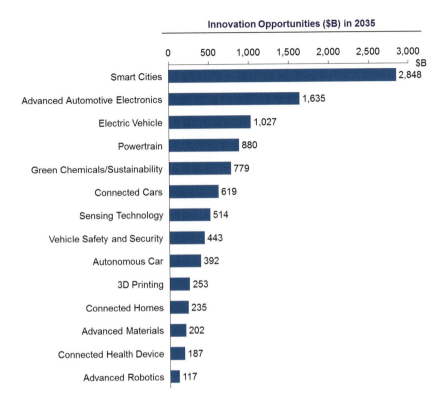

Figure 12.2 Top Innovation Areas and Future Revenue Opportunities.
Source: Lucintel.

sustainability, connected cars, advanced auto electronics, autonomous cars, connected homes, advanced robotics, advanced materials, connected health devices, and 3D printing.

Figure 12.1 shows the revenue opportunities for these top 14 innovations. Some, such as 3D printing, are applicable to multiple industries (construction, medical, automotive, and aerospace). The opportunities shown below are combined cross-industry totals.

Short-, medium- and long-term growth (horizon) potential is shown below (Table 12.1). This chart categorizes the top 14 innovations in terms of the Expanded Horizons Model[1] described in Chapter 1.

Definition of Each Innovation Type: Horizon 1 = Incremental, line extension, continuous improvement; **Horizon 2** = New to company or new to a sector; **Horizon 3** = Disruptive, new to the world.

Brief descriptions of these areas are provided below. For further details, please refer to previous relevant chapters.

150   Executing Your Strategy

Table 12.1 Horizon Model in Top 14 Innovation Areas

Areas of Innovation	Industry	Horizon 1	Horizon 2	Horizon 3
Smart cities	Construction, Electronics, Internet of Things (IoT)	Y	Y	Y
Powertrain advancement	Automotive	Y	Y	
Electric cars	Automotive	Y	Y	Y
Sensing technologies	Electronics	Y	Y	Y
Safety & security	Automotive	Y	Y	
Green chemicals/ sustainability	Chemical	Y	Y	
Connected cars	Automotive, IoT	Y	Y	Y
Advanced automotive electronics	Automotive, Electronics	Y	Y	Y
Autonomous cars	Automotive	Y	Y	Y
Advanced materials	Chemical	Y	Y	Y
Connected homes	Construction, IoT	Y	Y	Y
Advanced robotics	Electronics, automotive	Y	Y	Y
Connected health	Medical devices, IoT	Y		
3D printing	Construction, automotive	Y	Y	Y

Source: **Innovation**edge, LLC.
Content Source: Lucintel

Smart Cities: High Innovation Potential with $2,848 Billion Opportunities in 2035 with a CAGR of 11.4%

Smart cities are the integration of infrastructure with information and communication technology. This infrastructure provides efficiency and cost saving in healthcare, public transport, traffic, and energy management. The development of products and systems to increase energy efficiency and the growing need for public safety are driving factors. Security issues and lack of awareness are the key challenges (Table 12.2).

Powertrain Advancement: $880 Billion Opportunity in 2035

Automotive powertrain technology continues to advance. Advancements include increased efficiency of the traditional gasoline internal combustion engine, the use of turbocharging to make smaller

Summary **151**

Table 12.2 Areas of Innovation, Technologies, and Ecosystems in Smart Cities

Key Areas of Innovations	Technologies/ Solutions	Companies/Ecosystems
• Smart energy • Intelligent mobility • Smart security • Smart infrastructure • Smart education • Smart healthcare	• Smart meters • Smart traffic lights • Smart parking • Electric vehicle charging station	• GE • Huawei Investment & Holding Co., Ltd. • Cisco Systems • IBM Corporation • Microsoft Corporation • Oracle Corporation • Schneider Electric • Siemens AG • Ericsson, Hitachi Ltd. • Toshiba Corporation

Source: Lucintel.

Table 12.3 Areas of Innovation, Technologies, and Ecosystems in Powertrain Advancement

Key Areas of Innovation	Technologies/Solutions	Companies/ Ecosystems
• Advanced internal combustion engine concepts • Emissions after treatment modeling and control • Battery pack control and diagnostics • Electric powertrains • Improving energy efficiency using vehicle connectivity	• Development of hybrid engines • Increasing use of alternative fuels	• ZF Friedrichshafen AG • GKN Plc • BorgWarner INC • JTEKT Corp • GKN Plc • Borgwarner Inc.

Source: Lucintel.

displacement engines more powerful and efficient, the addition of more gears to the gearbox, and the use of lightweight materials in both vehicle bodies and engines. Rapidly changing power demands of electric, hydrogen, hybrid, and gas-powered vehicles and the availability of advanced energy-related technologies are drivers for this market. Lack of suitable high-voltage batteries and the high cost of hybrid vehicles are challenges (Table 12.3).

152 Executing Your Strategy

Electric Cars: $1,027 Billion Opportunity in 2035

Original equipment manufacturers (OEMs) are striving to reduce the weight and cost of the electric vehicles so that they are a viable and efficient choice for the customer. Government fuel economy standards, stringent greenhouse gas emissions rules, and the target to reduce harmful air pollution from exhaust emissions are the key factors driving the electric car market. Both the high cost associated with electric cars and limited infrastructure inhibits market growth (Table 12.4).

Sensing Technologies: $514 Billion Opportunity in 2035

Advanced sensing technologies are widely used to provide comfort, safety, process automation, and real-time data for various industries. Sensors support a variety of applications, from providing security to measuring health-related data. Increasing need for process, control, monitoring, and safety, and explosive growth in connected devices are the innovation drivers for the market (Table 12.5).

Vehicle Safety & Security: $443 Billion Opportunity in 2035

The automotive industry is changing rapidly to address the stringent requirements for safety and security of vehicular systems. An increase in the number of accidents and rising vehicle thefts are expected to fuel growth. The high cost of acquired technology is a key challenge associated with this market (Table 12.6).

Green Chemicals: $779 Billion Opportunity in 2035

Green chemicals will have a major impact on the environment and thus have high innovation opportunity. Companies are investing in R&D to

Table 12.4 Areas of Innovation, Technologies, and Ecosystems in Electric Cars

Key Areas of Innovation	Technologies/Solutions	Companies/ Ecosystems
• Wireless charging • **Development of efficient battery**	• Development of low-cost and lightweight batteries • Uses of graphene ball technology to increase battery capacity and reduce charging time	• Tesla • Chevrolet • Nissan

Source: Lucintel.

Summary 153

Table 12.5 Areas of Innovation, Technologies, and Ecosystems in Sensing Technologies

Key Areas of Innovation	Technologies/Solutions	Companies/Ecosystems
• Large area sensors • Low-power peripheral sensors • Energy harvesting sensors	• Radar, lidar • Ultrasonic sensor • Temperature/pressure sensor • Image and position sensor • Bio sensor • Level and flow sensor	• Pillar Technologies • Robert Bosch GmbH • Sony Corporation • STMicroelectronics • Analog Devices, Inc. • ABB Ltd. • Texas Instruments

Source: Lucintel.

Table 12.6 Areas of Innovation, Technologies, and Ecosystems in Safety and Security

Key Areas of Innovation	Technologies/Solutions	Companies/Ecosystems
• ADAS • Advanced fleet management • Smart transportation	• Emergency-braking system • Forward-collision warning • Adaptive cruise control	• Continental AG • ZF TRW • Delphi Automotive • Valeo SA

Source: Lucintel.

discover renewable sources of raw material to expand their renewable products portfolios. There is an increasing demand for bio-based polymers to reduce energy consumption, pollution, and VOC emissions, resulting in more eco-friendly products along with performance. The need for change in cost structure for bio-based products and raw materials is a constraint (Table 12.7).

Connected Cars: $619 Billion Opportunity in 2035

Automotive OEMs are developing a variety of new technologies that will make cars more digitally connected; for example, navigation systems that provide the fastest route to the driver. There is increasing demand for operational assistance, vehicle safety, and security (Table 12.8).

154   Executing Your Strategy

Table 12.7 Areas of Innovation, Technologies, and Ecosystems in Green Chemicals

Key Areas of Innovation	Technologies/Solutions	Companies/Ecosystems
• Bio-based polymers • Bioresin in UV coatings • Green coatings • Biodegradable polymers	• Development of UV curable bio-based products • Development of green coatings that contain antimicrobial properties	• BASF • Arkema • DSM • AkzoNobel • PPG

Source: Lucintel.

Table 12.8 Areas of Innovation, Technologies, and Ecosystems in Connected Cars

Key Areas of Innovation	Technologies/Solutions	Companies/Ecosystems
• ADAS	• Infotainment and navigation • Fleet management	• Continental AG • ZF TRW • Valeo SA • Robert Bosch Gmbh

Source: Lucintel.

Advanced Automotive Electronics: $1,635 Billion Opportunity in 2035

To reduce the possibility of accidents and increase safety, automobiles feature a set of functions called the advanced driver assistance functions. Integration of wireless and smartphone technology with available sensor and semiconductor solutions provides emergency assistance, vehicle-to-vehicle, and vehicle to infrastructure communication, along with infotainment. By 2020, the European Union and the United States have mandated that all vehicles come equipped with autonomous emergency-braking systems and forward-collision warning systems. Increasing demand for navigation services, assisted driving, vehicle speed, braking, transmission control systems are the key areas of innovation that will continue to grow as more countries stiffen regulations about vehicle safety. The absence of certifying bodies for standardization and regulations of the ADAS (advanced driver assistance systems)/telematics industry is one of challenges for this market (Table 12.9).

Table 12.9 Areas of Innovation, Technologies, and Ecosystems in Advanced Automotive Electronics

Key Areas of Innovation	Technologies/Solutions	Companies/Ecosystems
• ADAS	• Automatic emergency-braking system • Forward-collision warning • Adaptive cruise control	• Continental AG • Robert Bosch Gmbh • Delphi Automotive

Source: Lucintel.

Table 12.10 Areas of Innovation, Technologies, and Ecosystems in Autonomous Cars

Key Areas of Innovation	Technologies/Solutions	Companies/Ecosystems
• Autonomous systems	• Increasing innovations in software-based systems • Rapid progress in artificial intelligence	• Google • General Motors • Volkswagen • Tesla

Source: Lucintel.

Autonomous Cars: $392 Billion Opportunity in 2035

Autonomous vehicles (AVs) have the potential to transform mobility and society as AVs are predicted to reduce traffic incidents and associated fatalities and injuries and further improvements in the environment. By 2040, Lucintel expects that over 90% of all vehicles sold will be "Highly" and "Fully" autonomous systems, classified as Level 4 and 5 automation, while affordability and low cost will be a major catalyst to autonomous vehicle adoption. The major innovation drivers are reduced accidents, better traffic management, monitoring of other vehicles and pedestrians, and increased passenger comfort. The key challenges are high cost of infrastructure and regulation (Table 12.10).

Advanced Materials: $202 Billion Opportunity in 2035

Advanced materials have better properties than conventional materials, which are useful to reduce weight while withstanding higher operating temperatures and pressures. The automotive segment in the current scenario is focusing on weight reduction by replacing traditional materials. Lucintel expects increasing use of advanced materials such as titanium

156 Executing Your Strategy

aluminide, CMC, nano-composites, to be adopted in next-generation aircraft. Light in weight, higher strength, and excellent resistance to abrasion are key factors for the growth of the advanced materials market. High cost is a major challenge for the market (Table 12.11).

Connected Homes: $235 Billion Opportunity in 2035

Connected homes are the network of integrated multiple devices, service, and apps which enable remote home monitoring and control. Innovation drivers are the desire for greater comfort and convenience along with the need to reduce energy costs and crime rates. Complex technology and low awareness are the key challenges for this innovation (Table 12.12).

Table 12.11 Areas of Innovations, Technologies, and Ecosystems in Advanced Materials

Key Areas of Innovation	Technologies/ Solutions	Companies/Ecosystems
• Hybrid material • Usage of recycling materials • Usage of low-cost raw material to reduce the overall cost of the material	• Smart coating • Nano-material • Bio material	• 3M Advanced Materials • Morgan Advanced Materials plc • TATA Advanced Materials Limited

Source: Lucintel.

Table 12.12 Areas of Innovation, Technologies, and Ecosystems in Connected Homes

Key Areas of Innovation	Technologies/Solutions	Companies/ Ecosystems
• Home safety and security • Entertainment • HVAC control and smart lighting • Home appliance	• Connected appliances • Connected thermostats, smart lighting • Smart Entertainment • Connected lock, videos surveillance • Fire sprinklers and extinguishers • Intruder alarms	• Google • General Motors • Volkswagen • Tesla

Source: Lucintel.

Advanced Robotics: $117 Billion Opportunity in 2035

Advanced robotics are the devices which can interact physically with people and their environment and modify behavior based on sensor data. Advanced robotics can help decrease manufacturers' production costs while increasing flexibility to meet changing market needs. Technical challenges and high cost are constraints (Table 12.13).

Connected Health Devices: $187 Billion Opportunity in 2035

Connected health systems enable remote diagnoses, monitoring, and treatment by enabling access to patient-specific information from multiple sources. Digitalization and connectivity help realize today's emphasis on more efficient, patient-centric approaches while reducing cost, paperwork, and human error. They are especially helpful in monitoring and treating patients who are chronically ill, elderly, or housebound; the patient can be connected to a service network to assist in the case of emergencies as well. Finally, electronic health records (EHRs) allow doctors to pass along patient information to colleagues and specialists for consultation (Table 12.14).

3D Printing: $253 Billion Opportunity in 2035

3D printing is a manufacturing technique that builds objects layer by layer using materials such as polymers, metals, and composites. It is also known as additive printing technology and aids manufacturers in product and prototype development. Government investment in 3D printing projects and increased demand for customized products are drivers for this market. High production cost, lack of standard process control, and expensive software are constraints (Table 12.15).

Table 12.13 Areas of Innovation, Technologies, and Ecosystems in Advanced Robotics

Key Areas of Innovation	Technologies/Solutions	Companies/ Ecosystems
• Human-robot cooperative assembly • Nuclear facility inspection robots • Assisted living/elder care robots	• Sensing and perception • Human-robot interaction (HRI) • Intuitive interfaces • Modeling and simulation	• Softbank Robotics • Touch Bionics • iRobot

Source: Lucintel.

158 Executing Your Strategy

Table 12.14 Areas of Innovation, Technologies, and Ecosystems in Connected Health Devices

Key Areas of Innovation	Technologies/Solutions	Companies/Ecosystems
• Internet of things • mHealth technology • Wearables • Cloud	• Smart continuous glucose monitoring • Connected GPS • Cardio, fitness tracking • Remote diabetes management • At-home BP monitoring device	• Companies/Ecosystems • Medtronics • Omron • Fitbit • Roche Holding AG

Source: Lucintel.

Table 12.15 Areas of Innovation, Technologies, and Ecosystems in 3D Printing

Key Areas of Innovation	Technologies/Solutions	Companies/Ecosystems
• The printing welder • Speed printing	• Stereo-lithography • Selective laser sintering	• 3D Systems • Stratasys Ltd • The ExOne Company • Hoganas AB

Source: Lucintel.

Reference

1. **Innovation**edge, LLC., Expanded Horizons Model ©

Conclusion
Mapping Your Plan

Conclusion: Mapping Your Plan

Now that you have a complete picture of key success factors and emerging innovations, the big question is how do you connect your company's strategy and strengths with the right opportunities and partners? There are several ways you can develop a growth roadmap for your company from analyzing your core competencies and identifying opportunities to build-and-buy partner analysis. Here, we are presenting the **Innovation**edge Growth Opportunity Framework (IGOF)[1] to develop your organization's short- and long-term goals across four dimensions:

1. **Growth** into new markets, geographies, and technologies
2. **Competitive advantage,** organizational capability
3. **Financial value creation**
4. **Sustainable innovation** – balancing core, incremental, and breakthrough innovation

To develop your Innovation Engine for Growth it is important to create your framework by leveraging the steps below to Build Your Roadmap.[2]

Ten Key Action Steps

Strategy & Strengths

1. **Allocate resources across three horizons** based on your innovation ambition. Emphasize Horizons 2 and 3 for accelerated growth, but regardless of ambition, the largest share of resources is generally allocated to protect the core (Horizon 1).
2. **Consider megatrends** that are likely to impact your business. Look for potential opportunities in terms of markets, geographic expansion, and "white space."

DOI: 10.4324/9781003177906-18

160 Conclusion – Mapping Your Plan

3. **List potential areas of innovation** to focus on – what do your customers want today and in the future? What will offer meaningful, unique value?
4. **Create competency grids** to assess your organization's and potential partners' strengths. Identify synergies and gaps.
5. Identify the **capabilities** that form your **unique competitive advantage**.

Opportunities & Partners

6. **Note the three to five most attractive innovations** across all target industries.
7. **Identify areas of interest** aligned with megatrends and new emerging technology areas that complement your current business.
8. **Filter** by fit to your company's **long-term vision and mission. Further filter** by **market potential and market timing.** Refer to **Revenue Impact** section of each chapter for **market size** (CAGR through 2025), **revenue growth** (high, medium, low), and **technology readiness** within each category.
9. **Identify potential partners** and/or **ecosystems** that offer the specific innovations of interest.
10. **Create a short list** based on potential synergies and feasibility. (Further exploration will be necessary to assess risk/reward potential and cultural fit.)

Templates

The **IGOF**[1] is designed to focus your efforts on activities that generate maximum value, competitive advantage, and sustainable growth. The following templates can be used by your leadership team for strategic decision-making and planning:

1. Innovation Ambition
2. Team Competency Grid
3. Partner Competency Grid
4. Opportunity Impact/Ease
5. Opportunity Horizons
6. Innovation Value and Investment
7. Comparative Value
8. Innovation Growth Opportunity Matrix

Conclusion – Mapping Your Plan   161

Templates C.1–C.3 define your goals and core strengths as well as capabilities of potential partners. **Templates C.4–C.7** assess and compare the relative value of promising opportunities. **Template C.8** merges the assessments into a four-quadrant matrix with weighted values of opportunities across the four key dimensions.

	H1→	H2 →	H3
	1 year	2-4 yrs	5-10 yrs
	Incremental	New to company	New to the world
Accelerated	40%	40%	20%
Conservative	70%	20%	10%
Your ideal ratio			

Copyright Innovationedge 2020

Template C.1 Innovation Ambition
Source: **Innovation**edge, LLC.

Team Competencies
Rank each competency on a scale of 1-5, 5=superior.

	Processes/ Tools	Customer Insight	Service	Portfolio Management	External Collaboration	Internal Collaboration	Data Analytics	Technology Proficiency	Agile Development	Individual Total
Individual #1 Name										0
Individual #2 Name										0
Individual #3 Name										0
Individual #4 Name										0
Individual #5 Name										0
Individual #6 Name										0
Individual #7 Name										0
Individual #8 Name										0
Individual #9 Name										0
Individual #10 Name										0
Team total	0	0	0	0	0	0	0	0	0	0

Template C.2 Team Competency Grid
Source and Copyright: **Innovation**edge, LLC.

Partner Competencies
Rank each competency on a scale of 1-5, 5=superior.

	Processes/ Tools	Customer Insight	Service	Portfolio Management	External Collaboration	Internal Collaboration	Data Analytics	Technology Proficiency	Agile Development	Total
Partner A										0
Partner B										0
Partner C										0
Partner D										0
Our Company										0

Template C.3 Partner Competency Grid
Source and Copyright: **Innovation**edge, LLC.

162 Conclusion – Mapping Your Plan

		Relative Impact on Business	
		High	**Low**
Ease of Implementation	**Easy**	High Impact Easy to Implement	Low Impact Easy to Implement
	Not so Easy	High Impact Not so easy to Implement	Low Impact Not so easy to Implement

Copyright Innovaionedge 2020

Template C.4 Opportunity Impact/Ease Matrix
Source: **Innovation**edge, LLC.

Opportunity	H1	H2	H3
Opportunity A			
Opportunity B			
Opportunity C			
Opportunity D			
Opportunity E			

Template C.5 Opportunity Horizons
Source and Copyright: **Innovation**edge, LLC.

Innovation Ambition & Resource Allocation[3]

Innovation and growth depend on continuous feeding of the pipeline along with ongoing mechanisms to ensure projects are sufficiently re-sourced. H1 activities are usually managed with a gated process and projected return on investment (ROI) measures, and H3 activities have inherent unknowns which make investments purely speculative. Before evaluating opportunities, think about your organization's ambition – how far and how fast do you want to go? Does your current allocation need adjustment? Consider the full spectrum – number and time span of projects, degree of existing or to-be-acquired assets, risk tolerance, ROI, market growth, and game-changing potential. Use this chart to guide your decisions and choices. Your ratio can be 70/20/10, 60/25/15, 50/30/20 – the percentages depend on your objectives (Table C.1).

Conclusion – Mapping Your Plan   163

	Opp. A	Opp. B	Opp. C	Opp. D
Innovation Value				
Competitive advantage				
• Strategic importance				
• Alignment with core strengths				
• Intellectual Property (IP) value				
• Disruptive potential				
Subtotal	0	0	0	0
Market Attractiveness				
• Market size				
• Market growth				
• Technology feasibility/synergies				
Subtotal	0	0	0	0
Financial value creation				
• Short-term revenue				
• Long-term revenue				
Subtotal	0	0	0	0
Sustainable innovation				
• Aligns with ambition (H1, H2, H3 ratio)				
Subtotal	0	0	0	0
TOTAL INNOVATION VALUE	0	0	0	0
Innovation Investment				
• New capabilities needed (cost)				
• Market uncertainty				
• Capital investment				
Subtotal	0	0	0	0
TOTAL INNOVATION COST	0	0	0	0
NET VALUE	0	0	0	0

Conversion chart	Opp. A		Opp. B		Opp. C		Opp. D	
Competitive advantage	0	#DIV/0!	0	#DIV/0!	0	#DIV/0!	0	#DIV/0!
Market attractiveness	0	#DIV/0!	0	#DIV/0!	0	#DIV/0!	0	#DIV/0!
Financial value creation	0	#DIV/0!	0	#DIV/0!	0	#DIV/0!	0	#DIV/0!
Sustainable innovation	0	low	0	low	0	low	0	low
Total Innovation Cost	0	low	0	low	0	low	0	low
Net Innovation Value	0	low	0	low	0	low	0	low

Template C.6 Innovation Value and Investment
Source and Copyright: **Innovation**edge, LLC.

Innovation Growth Opportunity Matrix

Template C.7 Comparative Value
Source and Copyright: **Innovation**edge, LLC.

164 Conclusion – Mapping Your Plan

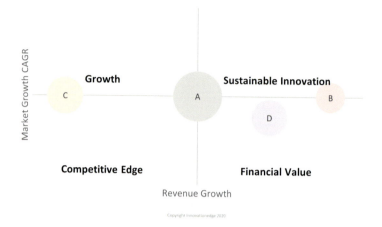

Template C.8 Innovation Growth Opportunity Matrix
Source: **Innovation**edge, LLC.

Table C.1 Innovation Ambition

	H1→	H2→	H3
	1 Year	2–4 Years	5–10 years
	Incremental	New to company	New to the world
Accelerated (%)	40	40	20
Conservative (%)	70	20	10
Your ideal ratio			

Source and Copyright: **Innovation**edge, LLC.

Competency Grids[4]

Competency grids include criteria ranging from behavioral and leadership competencies to specific technical competencies. Comprehensive grids allow senior leaders to evaluate individual and organizational performance from multiple perspectives, including performance related to specific programs, projects, or products.

Use the templates below to assess your organization's competencies as well as those of potential partners. The criteria listed in this example are drawn from Chapter 2; add or delete competencies based on your company's specific needs. **Rank each competency on a scale of 1-5, 5=superior.** Once you have created a competency grid for your own organization/team, the same template should be given to potential partners to construct their competency grids as well. Then each party should review,

Conclusion – Mapping Your Plan   165

discuss, and share examples and references that can validate the specific competencies identified. An example grid is shown below Template C.2

Team Competencies: Rank the competencies of each team member, sum the total for each individual. Then sum all the totals for an overall score of your team. High-scoring competencies will give you a picture of your core talents and strengths. Refer to the **Capability Building Blocks (Figure C.1)** to assess where you are on the Digital Innovation continuum.

An assessment of your organization's **technologies and assets** should be done on a separate worksheet; instead of individual's names, list your company's intellectual assets and rank their uniqueness (patents), feasibility (cost, readiness), and factors such as monetization potential, market share, and where they are in the product lifecycle.

Partner Competencies: This is a composite of potential partner strengths and competencies. Insert totals from each of their completed grids. On a separate row, enter your organization's total scores for each criteria as well as your overall score. This grid will show you relative strengths and weaknesses of potential partners so you can see which partners add important competencies that your organization currently lacks. Again, IP and technology assets will be on a separate worksheet.

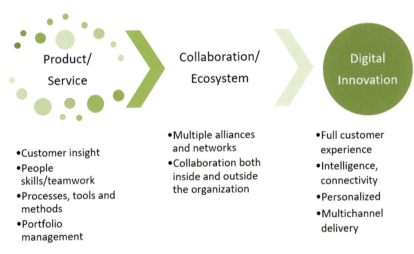

Figure C.1 Innovation Capability Building Blocks.
Source: **Innovation**edge, LLC.

Opportunity Identification and Valuation[5]

The next two sets of templates examine how different opportunities map to your organization's innovation ambition (**Horizon Mapping**)[6] and the comparative value they create (**Innovation Value Mapping**)[7] leveraging Innovationedge LLC's Expanded Horizons Model[8].

Horizon Mapping[6]

First, create a list of roughly five to eight attractive innovations based on their relevance to your opportunity discovery findings (Chapter 3). Map each into the following two horizon planning Templates C.4 and C.5:

1. **Opportunity Impact/Ease Matrix:** Those that are **high impact and easy to implement** are H1 and/or H2. **High impact and difficult to implement** are likely H3. Low-impact opportunities might be dropped altogether though ones that are **easy to implement could be H1.**
2. **Opportunity Horizons:** Use the grid below to map each opportunity's horizon potential based on **disruption potential, projected CAGR,** and **revenue growth** of industry (data provided in Chapters 5–11). This grid and the impact/ease matrix together help to choose short- and long-term opportunities.

Innovation Value Mapping[7]

The following two templates will assign values to each opportunity.

1. **Innovation Value and Investment:** The first spreadsheet lists ten **Innovation Value** criteria and three **Investment** criteria. First, rank each opportunity's criteria on a scale of **1-3**. (3=high, 2=medium, 1=low). Total the **Value.** Next, subtract the **Investment** (Innovation Cost) to calculate **Net Value.** Each member of your leadership team should complete this exercise independently and then discuss as a group to facilitate decision-making and alignment. This process will give you a comparative picture of all the opportunities.
2. **Comparative Value:** The next step is to enter the **subtotals** of the **four value dimensions** into the Comparative Value template.

Rank each opportunity's criteria on a scale of **1-3**. (3=high, 2=medium, 1=low)

Integrated Strategy/Opportunity Roadmap[9]

The final piece of the **IGOF**[1] integrates core strengths and external opportunities with revenue and market growth goals. **How it works:** Take the total values of each potential opportunity in each of the four dimensions. Based on the 1–3 scoring (low, medium, high) the **highest score** an opportunity can have in each dimension and their respective conversions are below:

Conversion Chart Illustration

Maximum Scores	Conversions
Competitive advantage = 12	1–4=low; 5–8=medium; 8–12=high
Market growth = 9	1–3=low; 4–6=medium; 7–9=high
Financial value creation = 6	1–2=low; 3–4=medium; 5–6=high
Sustainable innovation = 3	1=low; 2=medium; 3=high
Total innovation value = 30	1–10=low; 11–20=medium; 21–30=high
Innovation cost = 9	1–3=low; 4–6=medium; 7–8=high
Net innovation value = 27	1–19=low; 10–18=medium; 19–27=high

Source and Copyright: **Innovation**edge, LLC.

The low to high scores determine where promising opportunities fit on the four-quadrant matrix. Those closest to the center are highest on all four dimensions. Bubble size will correspond to the net innovation value of opportunity, as illustrated in the example below.

Case Example: Applying the Framework

To illustrate how the **IGOF**[1] works, we present a fictitious company called BevCo. BevCo makes and sells consumer beverages (primarily fruit juices, kids' juice boxes, sports drinks, and flavored waters); we purposely chose this example to demonstrate how the framework can be applied based on – and beyond – the seven industries discussed in Chapters 5–11. The example is simplified for the sake of brevity.

Background: BevCo is a publicly held company with steady finances. While it has enjoyed reasonably high market share (particularly in the kids' juice category), growth over the past few years has been sluggish. Innovations have been incremental such as sugar reduction, new flavor introductions, the addition of protein to sports drinks, and similarly conservative line extensions.

These innovations have kept BevCo in the game, but as the market becomes more saturated, retail shelf space is at a premium. Further, price competition and e-commerce are squeezing margins.

BevCo's senior leadership has decided the company needs to take bolder, bigger innovation risks to stay ahead. It is clear they will need external partners and/or suppliers to develop breakthrough products. The challenge is deciding where to invest time and resources and ensuring cross-functional alignment.

Innovation Ambition and Resource Allocation[3]

First, the leadership team (R&D, Marketing, Supply Chain, Operations, and Finance) reviewed their current product portfolio and pipeline. Like many consumer goods companies, they allocate most of their resources to the core. The company still plans to focus primarily on the core but invest more in future growth, particularly Horizon 2 (Table C.2).

Table C.2 Innovation Ambition and Resource Allocation

	H1→	H2→	H3
	1 year	2–4 years	5–10 years
	Incremental	New to company	New to the world
Current (%)	80	18	2
Goal (%)	70	25	5

Source and Copyright: **Innovation**edge, LLC.

Opportunity Identification[5] (Customer Insight & Megatrends)

The next critical step was to analyze customer input and feedback, purchasing behavior, loyalty, and demographics in conjunction with socio-economic megatrends (Chapter 4) (Figure C.2).

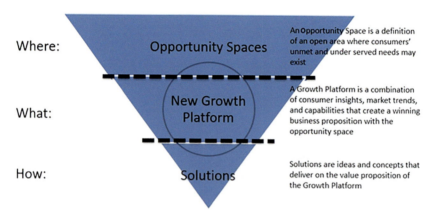

Figure C.2 Growth Platform Definition.
Source: **Innovation**edge, LLC.

Through the **Innovation**edge **Discovery Continuum Process**[10] and **Growth Platform Definition**[11] (Chapter 3), BevCo decided to focus on two key growth opportunity areas:

Green packaging – The megatrend is climate change, CO_2 emissions, and recyclability. BevCo customers have expressed concern about the otherwise popular juice boxes since they are made from composites that are potentially harmful to human health and the planet. The goal is to develop innovative, cost-effective solutions that also take into account shipping and shelf space constraints. One attractive option is **A) biodegradable polymers** which chapter 7 (Chemicals) identifies one of the highest growth opportunity areas with a CAGR of ~10% through 2025, strong technology readiness, and a number of qualified suppliers. Development would be possible within a two-year timeframe, making this a suitable H2 effort.

Another more 'breakthrough' option is **B) edible packaging** made from food waste. There are several companies and government-funded efforts to produce natural alternatives to bioplastics, including a project underwritten by the European Union to develop coatings from whey and potato proteins. The global market for these food-based alternatives is estimated to be growing by as much as 30% each year. BevCo is intrigued by the game-changing potential and creative design possibilities, but the timeframe is further out and the costs are not fully known. This would be an H2/H3 effort.

Functional beverages/nutraceuticals – The megatrend is consumer wellness and 'food as medicine,' particularly for the large and growing elder population. BevCo's initial concept is a line of **C) functional beverages** that promote better sleep, memory, energy, and mood, and lessen physical aches and pains. The 'secret sauce' would be **Cannabidiol (CBD)** which is known to help with anxiety, sleep, cognition, movement disorders, and pain. Clearly, there are regulatory hurdles and many unknowns, but CBD will undoubtedly be a competitive factor in the beverage industry going forward. BevCo needs to decide whether or not to be an early mover. This too would be an H2/H3 endeavor.

Competencies and Competitive Advantage[4]

Before deciding how to proceed with these three options, the leadership team assessed BevCo's core strengths to determine where it stands the best chance to win, and where it needs to partner or acquire. They filled out competency grids, did initial partnership screenings, and discussed their findings. Their internal strengths include customer insight, strong distribution channels, high product quality, and brand loyalty. Their main weaknesses are long cycle times and rigid processes. They

170   Conclusion – Mapping Your Plan

would seek sources where much of the early-stage development is completed, and where the partner brings such capabilities as Agile development to test concepts and prototypes with customers.

They concluded that all three options were attractive and aligned with their innovation ambition, strengths, and sourcing possibilities. **Biodegradable Packaging** was the most congruent with the goal to invest more in H2 activities (highest ease/impact).

Still, they felt they should explore the other two activities for their game-changing potential and long-term value. The question was which one; they could not afford to invest in both. Finally, they did an **Opportunity Valuation** analysis.

Opportunity Valuation[5]

Below is the result of their analysis. Opportunity A = Biodegradable polymers, Opportunity B = Edible packaging, Opportunity C = CBD infused beverages (Table C.3)

Table C.3 Growth Opportunity Matrix

	Opp. A	Opp. B	Opp. C	Opp. D
Innovation Value				
Competitive Advantage				
• Strategic importance	3	1	3	2
• Alignment with core strengths	3	1	3	1
• IP value	3	1		2
• Disruptive potential	3	1		1
Subtotal	**12**	**4**	**6**	**6**
Market Attractiveness				
• Market size	3	1	3	1
• Market growth	3	1	3	1
• Technology feasibility/ synergies	3	1		2
Subtotal	**9**	**3**	**6**	**4**
Financial Value Creation				
• Short-term revenue	3	3	1	3
• Long-term revenue	3	3		3
Subtotal	**6**	**6**	**1**	**6**

Conclusion – Mapping Your Plan

	Opp. A	Opp. B	Opp. C	Opp. D
Innovation Value				
Sustainable Innovation				
• Aligns with ambition (H1, H2, H3 ratio)	3	3	1	2
Subtotal	3	3	1	2
Total innovation value	30	16	14	18
Innovation Investment				
• New capabilities needed (cost)	1	2	3	1
• Market uncertainty	1	2	3	1
• Capital investment	1	2	3	2
Subtotal	3	6	9	4
Total innovation cost	3	6	9	4
Net value	27	10	5	14

Conversion Chart	Opp. A		Opp. B		Opp. C		Opp. D	
Competitive advantage	12	High	4	Low	6	High	6	med
Market attractiveness	9	High	3	Low	6	High	4	med
Financial value creation	6	High	6	High	1	Low	6	high
Sustainable innovation	3	High	3	High	1	Low	2	med
Total innovation cost	3	Low	6	Med	9	High	4	med
Net innovation value	27	**High**	10	Med	5	Low	14	med

Source and Copyright: **Innovation**edge, LLC.

The final bubble diagram shows a close race; the biggest bubble (highest net value) was **A** as expected. But **C** edged out **B** for its net value and competitive advantage potential (Figure C.3).

Figure C.3 **Innovation**edge Growth Opportunity Framework™ Matrix.
Source: **Innovation**edge, LLC.

172 Conclusion – Mapping Your Plan

So what did BevCo do? They proceeded with the Biodegradable Polymers project and dedicated a small amount of research funding to the CBD project. By using the **IGOF**, the leadership team was able to agree on priorities knowing they had systematically assessed and discussed the four key success dimensions.

Overall, these templates provide a timeless process that can be used repeatedly to evaluate new opportunities that arise. Technologies and markets change quickly; the power of the **IGOF** lies in its structure to organize information for decision-making and organizational alignment. The worksheets are modular and customizable – add and/or change criteria to suit different situations; use all templates for a holistic view or use individually for specific tasks and projects.

Remember, the templates are tools; your organization's growth depends on having a well-defined vision and strategy. Leadership, organizational culture, and commitment ultimately will determine success.

*The full set of interactive Innovationedge Growth Opportunity Framework worksheets with embedded formulas may be downloaded at Innovationedge.com or requested by email info@innovationedge.com.

References

1. Innovationedge, LLC., *Innovation*edge Growth Opportunity Framework™
2. Innovationedge, LLC., Build Your Roadmap ©
3. Innovationedge, LLC., Innovation Ambition and Resource Allocation ©
4. Innovationedge, LLC., Competency Grids ©
5. Innovationedge, LLC., Opportunity Identification and Valuation ©
6. Innovationedge, LLC., Horizon Mapping ©
7. Innovationedge, LLC., Innovation Value Mapping ©
8. Innovationedge, LLC., Expanded Horizons Model ©
9. Innovationedge, LLC., Opportunity Roadmap ©
10. Innovationedge, LLC., Discovery Continuum Process™
11. Innovationedge, LLC., Growth Platform Definition ©

Index

Note: **Bold** page numbers refer to tables; *italic* page numbers refer to figures.

ABB 128
accountants 20
ACTnano 87
Acuity Brands 121
adhesives 71, 75–76, 88, 89; structural 77, 89
Adient 66, 68
ADT 101, 121, 127–128
advanced automotive electronics 60, 61, 62–63, 64–65, 66, 69, 126, 154, **155**
advanced manufacturing processes: aerospace 51, 54, 56, 58; construction industry 92, 95, 97, 99, 100, 101, 102; *see also* 3D printing
aerospace 51–57, 107; aero engines 53, 54, 56, 58; aircraft health monitoring 54, 56–57; cleanliness 52, 57, 58; emerging innovations 51–54; highlights 56–57; Horizon planning 57–59; hybrid airships 53, 54, 56, 58; materials 51, 54–55, 56, 58, 59, 151–153; polymers 79; revenue impact and growth opportunities 54–57; safety 51, 52, 54, 55, 56–58
Africa 36, 39, 41
ageing population 33–34, 35–36, 132
agrochemicals 71, 72, 80–81, 82, 84, 86, 88, 90
Airbus 53, 54, 56, 126
AkzoNobel 71–72, 87
algorithms 18, 20; automotive industry 60
Alibaba Cloud Europe 111

alliance managers 30–31
alliances 29; *see also* partnerships
Allied Bioscience 57
Alphi 100
Alter G 141
Altran 56
Amazon 35, 115, 121
American Airlines 57
AMI 87
Apis Cor 95
Apple 122, 123, 128
Arcam AB 56
Arkema 86
artificial intelligence (AI) 18, 19, 20, 35, 44, 64, 66, 93, 114, 116, 118, 126, 129
Arup 93
A. Schulman 87
Asia 36, 37, 39, 41; *see also individual countries*
Asus 114
AT&T 121
automation and digitalization megatrends 35, 44, 45
automotive industry 60–69, 107; advanced automotive electronics 60, 61, 62–63, 64–65, 66, 69, 126, 154, **155**; airbags 64; autonomous vehicles 44, 60, 61, 62, 64–66, 67, 69, 149, 155; connected vehicles (*see* vehicles *under* connected); electric vehicles 60, 61, 63, 64, 65–66, 67, 69, 149, 150; emerging innovations 60–64; highlights 67–68; Horizon planning 68–69; materials 61, 67, 68–69, 155;

174 Index

polymers 78, 79, 87; powertrain advancement 60, 62, 64, 66, 68, 69, 149, 150–151; revenue impact and growth 64–68; safety and security 60, 63–64, 66, 68, 69, 149, 150, **151**; share mobility 60, 64–65, 66, 69

Bangladesh 36
banking 40, 116
BASF 77–78, 82, 86, 87, 88, 101
battery technology 35, 41, 45, 61, 65, 67, 69, 123, 131, 137
Bayer Crop Science 81, 86
behavioral science 18
big data 56, 104, 109–110, 112, 115, 116
bio-plasticizers 78, 87, 89–90
biodegradable 73; implants 106; packaging 77–78, 86–87, 89, 169, 170; polymers 71, 72, 78, 89, 169, 172
biofuels 81, 84, 90
Biotricity 133
BMW 61, 67
Boeing 52, 54, 56, 119, 126
BorgWarner 68
Bosch 60, 62–63, 66, 68, 101, 127
Brazil 34, 36, 37, 39
breakthrough innovation 7; Horizon 3 (see separate entry)
building see construction industry
business growth partners 20

Cambridge Medical Robotics 140
Cambridge Polymers 74
Canada 34, 37
cancer 139
capabilities 23, 147; collaborative innovation 16, 19, 22, 23; digital innovation 16, 19–20, 22, 23; product/service innovation 16, 17–19, 23
capital markets 12
CFM International 56
change management 31
chemical industry 71–90; agrochemicals 71, 72, 80–81, 82, 84, 86, 88, 90; coatings 71, 72–75, 82, 84, 86, 87, 89; emerging innovations 71–81; green chemicals/sustainability 71–78, 86–87, 89–90,

149, 150–151, **154**; highlights 86–88; Horizon planning 88–90; polymers 71, 75–80, 82, 84, 86, 87, 88, 89–90, 169; revenue impact and growth 82–88
Chevrolet 67
China 34, 35–36, 37, 39; climate change 42, 44, 45
Cisco Systems 121, 128
cities: smart (see separate entry); sustainable 95–97
Clariant 81
cleaning supplies businesses 14
cleanliness 33, 119; aerospace 52, 57, 58
climate change 35, 42–44, 45, 169; aerospace 53; automotive industry 61, 65; biofuels 81; construction industry 100; electronics 107–108
cloud computing 20, 104, 109, 110–111, 112, 114, 116, 124, 129; aerospace 56; construction industry 101; infrastructures as a service (IaaS) 111; medical devices 136, 140, 142
collaborative innovation: capabilities 16, 19, 22, 23; opportunity discovery for 26–27
Collodin 101
communication strategy 18–19
competencies 23, 24; case study 169–170; due diligence 30; grids 29, 30, 161, 164–165, 169; potential partners 29–30, 31, 161, 164–165
competitive position 2, 5, 9, 10, 14
connected: health 35, 40, 125, 132–133, 137–138, 139–140, 141, 149, 157, **158**; homes 35, 40, 101, 114, 118, 119–120, 125, 126, 127–128, 129, 149, 156; vehicles 35, 40, 61, 63, 64–65, 108, 118, 119, 123–124, 125, 126, 128, 129, 149, 151, **154**; wearables 118, 122–123, 125, 126, 128, 129, 137
construction industry 92–103; building information modeling (BIM) 93; design for compact spaces 95–97, 97, 99, 101, 102; emerging innovations 92–97; green buildings 92, 94, 97, 99, 100–101, 102; highlights 100–101; Horizon planning 101–103; materials 92, 93,

94, 95, 99, 100–101, 102; polymers 78, 79; revenue impact and growth 97–101; smart building examples 93; *see also* smart homes
contact lenses 119, 122
Continental AG 66
Contour Crafting Corporation 95
Control4 Corporation 121
coopetition 25
COVID-19 2–3, 8, 25, 49, 148; aerospace 54, 57, 58; automotive industry 64; capabilities 16; chemical industry 82; construction industry 97; electronics 112; flexibility 18; healthcare 33, 45–46, 106, 138; Internet of Things (IoT) 126; opportunity discovery process 27–28; resource allocation 14; robots 106, 138; self-manage 18; touchless/low touch economy 3, 33, 35, 116, 126
Critical Manufacturing 137
critical skills 19–20
critical success factors 147–148
cross-generational management 17–18
customer insight 18, 20, 46, 168–169
customer relationship management (CRM) 19
CyBe Construction 95

D-Link Europe 119–120, 122
data analytics 18, 19–20, 109–110, 115; aerospace 56
data science 20
definition of innovation 7
Deka Research & Development 135
Delphi Automotive 68
demographic and population megatrends 33–34, 36, 103, 116
Denso Corporation 66
design for compact spaces 95–97, 97, 99, 101, 102 design for compact spaces 95–97, 97, 99, 101, 102
design thinking 12, 18
developing countries 41, 78
digital innovation capabilities 16, 19–20, 22, 23
digitalization and automation megatrends 35, 44, 45
disabilities 119
DJO Global Inc. 141
Dow 73, 77, 82, 88, 101

drones 106
DSM 86
DuPont 88
Duravit 96–97, 101

Eastern Europe 39
economic power shifts 34, 36–39
economies of scale 29
Ekso Bionics 141
electric vehicles 60, 61, 63, 64, 65–66, 67, 69, 149, 150
electronics 104–117, 131, 132; advanced display technology 104–105, 112, 114, 115; big data 104, 109–110, 112, 115, 116; chemical industry: coatings 74, 87, 89; emerging innovations 104–111; energy-efficient technologies 102, 107–108, 112, 114, 116; flexible hybrid 105–106, 112, 116; highlights 114–115; Horizon planning 115–116; miniaturization 108–109, 112, 114, 116, 137; personal robots 106–107, 111, 112, 114–115, 116; polymers 78, 79; revenue impact and growth 111–115; smart implants with integrated 139, 140
Embraer Commercial Aviation Ltd 52
emerging markets 34, 36–39, 45
employee recruitment 19–20
energy: -efficient technologies 102, 107–108, 112, 114, 116; megatrends 35, 40–42, 45; renewable 35, 41–42, 43, 121
environment: aerospace 53; *see also* climate change; green buildings; green chemicals/sustainability
Ericsson 121
Europe 39, 41, 61, 64, 67, 78, 120; *see also individual countries*
European Union 45, 154, 169; aerospace 53; climate change 42, 43–44, 45, 53
ExOne Company 56
experimental learning 28

failures 18, 23, 28, 145
Fastbrick 92
Faurecia 66, 68
Fitbit 122, 123, 128, 139
5G 111, 112, 119

Flipkart 35
Ford 60, 61, 64, 65–66, 67, 126
40-40-20 ratio 15
France 34, 37

GAF 101
GE 56, 126, 128, 141
General Motors (GM) 61, 64, 65–66, 67
genomics 132
Geon Performance Materials 78
Germany 34, 37
GKN 51, 56, 68
global process owners 20
Google 12, 26, 61, 65, 67, 121, 122, 123, 128
green buildings 92, 94, 97, 99, 100–101, 102
green chemicals/sustainability 71–78, 86–87, 89–90, 149, 150–151, **154**
gross domestic product (GDP) 37–39
Growth Platform Definition 27–28, 169

healthcare 3, 106, 107, 109, 116; connected health (*see* health *under* connected); connected wearables 122, 123, 128, 129, 137; electronic health records 132–133; flexible hybrid electronics 106, 112; Internet of Things (IoT) 119, 123, 129; medical devices (*see separate entry*); megatrends 33, 35–36, 45–46, 169
Hikvision 120–121
Hitachi 121
homes: connected (*see* homes *under* connected); micro apartments/tiny 96–97, 99; security and surveillance systems 119–120; smart (*see separate entry*)
Honeywell 51, 101, 121, 126, 127, 128
Hong Kong 99
Horizon 1 8–9, *11*, 12–14, 15, 18; aerospace 57–59; automotive industry 68–69; case example: applying IGOF 167–172; chemical industry 88–90; construction industry 101–103; electronics 115–116; Internet of Things (IoT) 128–129; medical devices 141–142;

templates 162–164, 166; top innovation areas 149, **150**
Horizon 2 8, 9–10, *11*, 12–14, 15, 18; aerospace 57–59; automotive industry 68–69; case example: applying IGOF 167–172; chemical industry 88–90; construction industry 101–103; electronics 115–116; Internet of Things (IoT) 128–129; medical devices 141–142; templates 162–164, 166; top innovation areas 149, **150**
Horizon 3 8, 10, 11, 12–14, 15, 18; aerospace 57–59; automotive industry 68–69; case example: applying IGOF 167–172; chemical industry 88–90; construction industry 101–103; electronics 115–116; Internet of Things (IoT) 128–129; medical devices 141–142; templates 162–164, 166; top innovation areas 149, **150**
Huawei 121
Huntsman 100, 101

IBM 121, 128
imperfection 28
incremental innovation 7; Horizon 1 (*see separate entry*)
India 34, 36, 37, 39; climate change 42, 44, 45
Indonesia 34, 36, 37, 39
industrial manufacturers: resource allocation 13
information 26–27; external networks 28; integration and management of 18; Internet connectivity 108; sensors 107; *see also* big data
Innovation Ambition Matrix 12, *13*
Innovationedge Discovery Continuum Process 26–27, 169
Innovationedge Growth Opportunity Framework[TM] (IGOF) 2, 22, 159; case example 167–172; competencies and competitive advantage 169–170; competency grids 29, 30, 161, 164–165, 169; innovation ambition and resource allocation 162–164, 168; integrated strategy/opportunity roadmap 166–167; opportunity identification (customer insight and megatrends)

166, 168–169; opportunity valuation 166, 170–171; templates 160–164, 166
inspection: aerospace 51–52, 57
insurance 36, 65, 109, 116, 123, 124
intellectual property (IP) 3, 22, 27, 30
Intelligent Implants 140
Internet 34–35, 39–40, 45, 108, 112, 114, 116
Internet of Things (IoT) 3, 34–35, 39–40, 44, 112, 118–130; 5G 111, 119; aerospace 5; cloud-based 111; emerging innovations 118–125; energy 41; Horizon planning 128–129; industrial 114, 119, 124, 125, 126, 128, 129; medical devices 131; Micro-Electro-Mechanical Systems (MEMS) 109; revenue impact and growth 125–128
Intuitive Surgical 140
Italy 34, 37

J & J Flooring 100, 101
Japan 34, 36, 99
Johns Manville 100–101
Johnson & Johnson 121, 131

Knauf 101
Kone 101

LANXESS 87
Latin America 39; Brazil 34, 36, 37, 39; Mexico 34, 37
leadership 23
Leaf Resources 72
Lear 66, 68
LG 104–105, 114
LyondellBasell 82

machine learning 18, 20, 35, 44, 110, 118
Magna International 66
mapping your plan 159–172; Innovationedge Growth Opportunity Framework^{TM} (IGOF) (*see separate entry*)
market research 18
MarkLogic 109–110
materials, advanced 149, 155–156; aerospace 51, 54, 56, 58, 61, 155–156; automotive industry 61, 67, 68–69, 155; chemical industry

87, 90; construction industry 92, 93, 94, 95, 99, 100–101, 102
Mayfield Robotics 114
medical devices 131–142; chemical industry: coatings 74, 87, 89; connected health (*see* health *under* connected); emerging innovations 131–137; highlights 139–141; Horizon planning 141–142; miniaturization/portability 137, 138, 139, 141, 142; minimally invasive and robotic surgery 131–132, 133–134, 138, 139, 140, 141; prosthetics 132, 135–136, 137–138, 139, 141, 142; real time diagnostic and monitoring 132, 136, 138, 139, 141, 142; smart implants 132, 134–135, 137–138, 139, 140, 141, 142; smart probes 139
Medtronic 128, 139, 140
megatrends 3, 6, 23, 33–46, 103, 116, 148, 168–169
mentorship 17–18, 23
Mercedes-Benz 60–61
mergers and acquisitions (M & A) 3, 16, 19, 23, 82
Mexico 34, 37
Micro-Electro-Mechanical Systems (MEMS) 109
Microsoft 121
Middle East 41
miniaturization 108–109, 112, 114, 116; medical devices 137, 138, 139, 141, 142
mobile phones/smartphones 10, 40, 45, 101, 105–106, 108, 114, 115, 120, 122, 127–128, 140, 141, 154, 156
Monsanto 86
Multek 112

Nagji, B. 12, 13
nanotechnology 69, 72, 82, 84, 88; healthcare 132; nano-coatings 64, 84, 87, 89; nano-composites 56, 156; nano-fillers 77, 84, 89; nano-pesticides 71, 72, 80, 84, 90
natural gas 41
NatureWorks 86–87
New Relic 115
Nigeria 36
Nike 122

178 Index

Nissan 67
North America 37, 39, 41, 78; Canada 34, 37; Mexico 34, 37; United States (*see separate entry*)
not-invented-here (NIH) syndrome 31

Oceania 39
Omron 128, 139
open innovation 25, 28–29
opportunity: discovery for collaborative innovation 26–28; identification 20, 22–23, 168–169
Oracle 121
organizational change 30–31
organizational culture 30
Ori 99
original equipment manufacturers (OEMs) 77, 87, 90; aerospace 53, 54, 56; automotive industry 60, 61, 64, 66, 67, 87, 123, 150, 151
OrthoSensor 136
Ossur Corporate 141
Otto Block Inc. 141
outsourcing 29
Owens Corning 100, 101

packaging: chemical industry 72, 73, 76, 77–78, 86–87, 89, 169, 170; edible 169; green 72, 77–78, 169
Pakistan 36
pandemic *see* COVID-19
partnerships 19, 23; strategic 25–32
people skills 17–18
Philips 121, 141
pipeline management 12
pitfalls to avoid: partnerships 30
plan *see* mapping your plan
population and demographic megatrends 33–34, 36, 103, 116
portfolio management 19, 21–23, 31
powertrain advancement 60, 62, 64, 66, 68, 69, 149, 150–151
PPG 87
Pratt & Whitney 56
product/service innovation capabilities 16, 17–19, 23
prosthetics, advanced 132, 135–136, 137–138, 139, 141, 142

RAK Ceramics 101
Recaro 57
recyclable paper coating 73, 87, 89

reframing 27
renewable energy 35, 41–42, 43, 121
resource allocation: 72-20-10 rule 12–14, 15; adjustments 14, 15; extent of innovation/ambition and risk 12; pipeline management 12
Resource Furniture 101
retail 109, 120–121
return on investment (ROI) 2, 11, 12, 100, 162; research and development 66
ReWalk Robotics 141
Rex Bionics Ltd 141
risk 28, 29, 31, 145; and reward 12, 22; tolerance 12, 19, 30, 31, 162
roadmap 15, 24, 32, 45–46, 159–161
robotics 35, 44, 107, 112, 124, 125, 149, 157; aerospace 51, 58; automotive industry 66; construction industry 92, 95, 99, 102; COVID-19 106, 138; medical devices 106, 107, 131–132, 133–134, 135, 138, 139, 140, 141; personal robots 106–107, 111, 112, 114–115, 116
Roca 100
Roche 139–140
Rolls-Royce 54, 56
RTP Company 87
Russia 34, 36, 37

SABIC 79–80, 87
safety 33, 44; aerospace 51, 52, 54, 56–59; automotive industry 60, 63–64, 66, 68, 69, 149, 150, **151**; construction industry 93
Safran 126
Saint Gobain 101
Samsung 114, 132
Sanwa 101
Schneider Electric 121, 128
seed treatment 81, 84, 90
SEMI FlexTech 106
sensing technologies 35, 44, 104, 106, 107, 111–112, 114, 116, 149, 150, **151**; aerospace 57, 107; automotive industry 63, 64, 107; chemical industry 80; Internet of Things (IoT) 118, 119, 123, 124, 126, 129; medical devices 107, 131, 134, 136, 137, 141, 142; radar and lidar 107, 116

service/product innovation capabilities 16, 17–19, 23
70-20-10 rule 12–14, 15
Sherwin-Williams 75
Siemens AG 121
Sika 88
skills, critical 19–20
smart cities 100, 114, 118, 119, 121, 125, 126, 128, 129, 149, 150, **151**
smart grids 107–108, 116
smart homes 3, 108, 120, 121, 122, 126; construction industry 94, 97, 99, 101, 102
smart implants 132, 134–135, 137–138, 139, 140, 141, 142
smart meters 107, 116
smart probes 139
smartphones *see* mobile phones/smartphones
socio-economic class 40
Softbank Robotics 114
Solvay 87
Sony 114
Sphera Solutions 122
Splunk Enterprise 115
stage of development 14
Stratasys Ltd 56
strategic partnerships 25–32
strategy and vision 20, 22–23
strengths 20, 23, 24, 147
surgery, minimally invasive and robotic 131–132, 133–134, 138, 139, 140, 141
sustainability/green chemicals 71–78, 86–87, 89–90, 149, 150–151, **154**
sustainable cities 95–97
sustaining innovation 7; Horizon 2 (*see separate entry*)
Syngenta 86, 88

Tableau 115
Tarkett 100, 101
teamwork 18, 23
Tech Mahindra 56
technology companies: resource allocation 14
templates 162–164, 166
Tesla 61, 65, 67, 121, 128
Three Horizon Framework 5, 7–15, 23, 49, 147; case example: applying

IGOF 167–172; Horizon 1 (*see separate entry*); Horizon 2 (*see separate entry*); Horizon 3 (*see separate entry*); platform model 10–11; resource allocation 12–14, 15; spanning the horizons 10–12; summary 15; templates 162–164, 166; *see also* mapping your plan
3D printing 149, 157, **158**; aerospace 51, 56; construction industry 92, 95, 97, 99, 100, 101, 102; medical devices 131–132, 134, 135, 136
Toshiba 121, 141
TOTO 101
Toyota Motors 66, 67
TransEnterix 140
transformation leaders 20
Tuff, G. 12, 13
Turkey 34, 37

UBTECH Robotics 115
United Airlines 57, 58
United Kingdom 34, 37
United States 34, 35, 36, 37, 99, 120, 139; climate change 42, 43, 45
United Technologies Corporation 121
UPS 124–125
urbanization 95, 103; *see also* cities
USG 101
UTC Aerospace Systems 54

Vilinger 57
vision and strategy 20, 22–23
Vivint 101, 121, 127
Volkswagon 61, 65–66, 67, 128
Volvo 64, 67
VT Miltope 56

Wanderwash 101
WaveLynx Technologies Corporation 101
wearables, connected *see* wearables *under* connected
wellness 33, 36, 46, 68, 141, 169
William McDonough Partners 93

Yirego 101

ZF TRW 66, 68

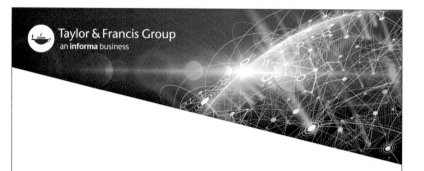